Grilling

Grilling

Mary B. Johnson

STERLING
INNOVATION
A Division of Sterling Publishing Co., Inc.
New York

The Library of Congress has cataloged the original edition as:
Johnson, Mary B.
  Grilling/ by Mary B. Johnson
    p. cm. – (Quick cooks' kitchen)
  ISBN 0-7607-5750-X
  1. Barbecue cookery. I. Title. II. Series.

TX840.B3J66 2005
641.7'6–dc22   2004062701

2 4 6 8 10 9 7 5 3 1

Published by Sterling Publishing Co., Inc.
387 Park Avenue South, New York, NY 10016
This book was originally published as *Quick Cooks' Kitchen: Grilling*

© 2005 by Sterling Publishing Co., Inc.
Photographs © 2005 by Theresa Raffetto

Distributed in Canada by Sterling Publishing
c/o Canadian Manda Group, 165 Dufferin Street
Toronto, Ontario, Canada M6K 3H6
Distributed in the United Kingdom by GMC Distribution Services
Castle Place, 166 High Street, Lewes, East Sussex, England BN7 1XU
Distributed in Australia by Capricorn Link (Australia) Pty. Ltd.
P.O. Box 704, Windsor, NSW 2756, Australia

Design by Liz Trovato
Photographs by Theresa Raffetto
Food Stylist: Victoria Granof
Prop Stylist: Dominique Baynes

Thanks to the Palmers for use of their seaside location.

Sterling ISBN-13: 978-1-4027-4347-4
ISBN-10: 1-4027-4347-5

For information about custom editions, special sales, premium and
corporate purchases, please contact Sterling Special Sales
Department at 800-805-5489 or specialsales@sterlingpub.com.

Contents

Introduction

With so many options for a quick meal—quality frozen, prepared, and ready-to-heat foods; take-out and delivery; and microwavable everything—there seems to be little reason to cook! *Grilling* provides you with over 150 recipes that are full of home-cooked goodness to satisfy the hurried chef in all of us.

Grilling foods is not just for the weekend barbecue; these recipes can be done quickly enough to have a tasty dinner on the table on a busy weeknight, without losing any of the great taste of grilled foods. Better yet, the recipes in *Grilling* go beyond the basic hamburgers, hot dogs, and steaks. Quesadillas, salads, tacos, and even pizzas can all be prepared on the grill.

Cooks' Tips

Throughout these pages you will come across shortcuts, hints, and tips that are designed to help you. Here is some general advice to always consider when you are cooking:

• Always read the recipe from start to finish before beginning your preparation. Make sure you understand the directions and reread anything that seems unclear to you.

• Start by getting all your ingredients within reach and do all your prep work before beginning to cook.

Grill Basics

Barbecuing, grilling, and broiling are technically different but have ultimately the same result: Food is cooked over or under an exposed heat source (charcoal, a wood fire, gas-grill coals, or a searing coil of gas flames or electric heat) until cooked to the desired doneness. In this book, the term "grill" is used for the cooking method.

How High the Heat

In most grilling there is some control of the heat exposed to the food or the food exposed to the heat:

1. Directly, by controlling the intensity of the flames or the number of gas lines on a gas grill, or by using more or less charcoal;

2. By venting the gas or charcoal grill (a science in itself);

3. By moving the food toward or away from the heat source.

Grilling Equipment

• Keep the grill clean. Buy 3 or 4 wire grill brushes at the beginning of the summer. When the first one gets coated with grease and burnt food, throw it out and use a new one. You will be more motivated to clean the grill rack before each use if the brush isn't dirty or falling apart.

- Buy heavy work gloves to wear when cleaning the grill and grill racks. The wire on the grill brush hurts like heck when it pricks you, so you want to protect your hands as well as your fingernails.

- Buy grill-safe utensils with hardwood handles. Plastic handles will melt if put too close to the heat.

- Buy sturdy utensils. You need to be able to safely support the cooked foods, which can be surprisingly hot and heavy.

- Use long-handled tongs for turning the food. Use tongs with rounded ends, not spiked ones, so foods such as tomatoes will not break when squeezed.

- Use a sturdy long-handled spatula for turning food or a combination of tongs and a spatula.

- Do not use a fork to turn food. The prongs will cause the juices and fat to gush out into the fire, drying out the meat and causing smoke and flames.

- Use a long-handled brush for oiling the grill and applying marinade.

- Invest in wire grill baskets and racks. Vegetable baskets and hinged racks for burgers, fish, and chicken parts are great for moving ingredients on, off, and around the grill in one fell swoop and are handy when it's time to turn the food.

- Place a clean table near the grill. You will be able to set up your flow of work for maximum efficiency and safety.

- Have a sturdy squirt bottle of water ready to put out flame-ups. Be sure it is set to fire directly on the flame and not set to spray a wide mist, which would drench the food.

- Buy several pairs of heavy, long oven mitts a season for use near the grill as they will no doubt get holes burned in them and coated with grease and marinades. Be sure the palm side is insulated so you can work over the grill and not burn yourself or the mitt.

- Wash tools with hardwood handles by hand. They won't dry out and crack if dried right away. Make sure brushes are washed thoroughly in hot, soapy water.

Greasing the Racks

- After cleaning the grill racks, brush them with a neutral-flavored vegetable oil and place on the grill.

- You can tell if your rack needs re-oiling by flicking a few drops of water onto a hot grill. If the water evaporates quickly and does not bead up, it's time to grease.

- If using nonstick cooking spray, do not spray the rack while it is on the grill, when the grill is being heated, or if it is hot. Apply the spray to the grill rack in a well-ventilated place and place it on the grill.

Preheating the Grill

- Turn on a gas grill, allowing 10 to 15 minutes to become medium hot.

● Charcoal Cooking: For a clean flavor, use hardwood charcoal, not pre-soaked, ready-to-light briquets. Twist some newspaper into 5-inch coils and place in a charcoal chimney (a large metal can or pipe-like container with vents at the bottom and a heat-safe handle). Add 30 to 50 briquets (enough to line a 22 1/2-inch grill and cook enough food for a meal) and ignite. About 20 minutes later, when the coals are red-hot, spread out the coals in a single layer in the grill, leaving about 4 inches of space in one area for a "cool zone" and place the grill rack on top. When a white ash forms on the coals, they are ready to test.

GRILLING TEMPERATURES

If your grill does not have a thermometer, here's a way to estimate the heat of the grill: Hold your hand palm side down about 2 feet above the heat source or coals. So that your hand is not suddenly exposed to high heat, bring down your hand in 6-inch increments until it is about 12 inches from the heat source. Calculate the heat by counting how long you can hold your hand above the heat by starting with "one Mississippi," "two Mississippi," etc. Here's the scale to obtain the approximate temperature of the heat:

Number of seconds	Heat of the fire	Approximate temperature °F
1 (or less)	very hot	600° or above
2	hot	500° to 650°
3	medium hot	450° to 550°
4	medium	400° to 500°
5	medium low	300° to 400°
6 (or more)	low	300° or below

Basic Food Safety

● Defrost frozen ground meat or steaks in the refrigerator, not at room temperature. Allow 12 to 24 hours to defrost 1- to 1 1/2-inch thick steaks or patties.

● Wash hands, the counter, platter, utensils, and containers with hot, soapy water before and after contact with raw meat.

● Do not place cooked meat onto dishes, cutting boards, or platters that have not been cleaned after holding raw meat.

Flavored Brines

Salt water is often used to cure or preserve meats; a short-term flavoring brine is a quick way to season and moisten meats, usually pork, for grilling. There are several recipes of flavor mixes in this book, but here are the general ratios of brine to meat and timing guidelines:

● Use about 2 tablespoons to 1/4 cup flavored brine (brine ratio: 2 teaspoons salt to 1 cup water) for injecting each 1 to 2 pounds of pork chops at least 1 1/4 inches thick. Injected meat can be cooked immediately or refrigerated up to 2 hours.

● Use about 2 cups light brine (brine ratio: 2 teaspoons salt to 1 cup water) to soak 2 to 3 pounds of pork chops or tenderloins for 4 to 6 hours in the refrigerator. (Soak a butterflied pork tenderloin only up to 2 hours.)

● Brined pork will have a pink color even if it is cooked to maximum doneness, 150° F.

Rubs

Dry spices applied to the oiled surface of meat, fish, and poultry before grilling offer the cook quick options with maximum flavor results. Purchased spice mixes or your own "house" blends usually contain some salt, so the meat can go from grill to table and you won't have any last-minute seasoning to remember to do. The general guideline is:

● Use 1 to 2 teaspoons pungent spice rub for each serving of meat or poultry.

Marinating

● Marinate meat, fish, and poultry only for 15 to 20 minutes at room temperature, the amount of time it would take for it to begin to get the chill off it anyway.

● To keep acidic ingredients from reacting with metal, marinate meat in a plastic food storage bag or a glass, plastic, or other non-reactive container.

● Use about 1/2 to 3/4 cup mild marinade for each 1 to 2 pounds of food.

● Use about 1/4 to 1/2 cup sweet or strong marinade for each 1 to 2 pounds of food.

● Turn or stir marinating pieces of food every 5 minutes.

● Tender cuts of meat and delicately flavored fish and poultry need only about 15 minutes to obtain good flavor from a marinade.

● Tougher cuts of meat are best cooked slowly, for relatively long periods of time, so they are not used in the recipes in this book.

● Drain marinade off food as much as possible before cooking to keep marinade from dripping into the fire and then flaming and smoking. A wet surface is also slow to sear and seal, so marinated food may overcook or steam before a nice glaze forms.

● Stop basting meat with its marinating juices the last 2 minutes of grilling so any marinade (and the meat, fish, or poultry juices in it) is cooked thoroughly.

Using an Instant-Read Thermometer

● Remove thermometer from its protective pocket-clamp and insert horizontally mid-way into a burger or steak, without touching any bone or fat, or the grill.

● Allow thermometer ascent to reach a steady final motion that fluctuates only one or two degrees. Observe the movement for 10 to 15 seconds and then register the internal temperature at the steadiest point.

● Steaks: Doneness for medium rare is at least 145° F.

● Lamb is medium rare when the thermometer registers 150° F.

● Cook pork to a maximum of 150° F (do not go by color as brined pork is pink when done).

● Beef burgers are "medium" doneness when thermometer registers at least 160° F and meat and juices are not pink.

● Cook white meat chicken to at least 170° F, until the flesh is opaque, not pink; thighs should cook to at least 180° F.

Grilling Sense

• Trim off the excess fat from meat and poultry before cooking to prevent flare-ups during cooking.

• Baste carefully and neatly to prevent the sauce from dripping into the fire.

• Apply sugary glazes to food just before removing from the grill. Allow enough time for the glaze to set, but be alert as it can burn quickly.

• Don't press on burgers, chops, or steaks with a spatula. This will squeeze out the juices.

• Give grilled meat and poultry a rest after cooking. Place the hot food on a warm platter or cutting board with a deep trench in it and cover loosely with foil. Let stand at least 5 minutes before serving. This will give the juices that have been driven into the center of the food time to flow back into the surface areas.

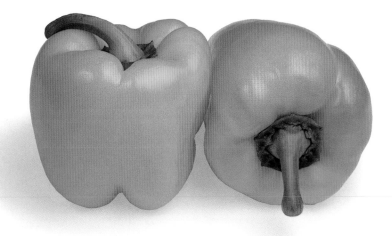

Appetizers

PREP TIME: 20 MINUTES   COOKING TIME: 12 MINUTES

Grilled Eggplant Bruschetta

MAKES 4 SERVINGS

Eggplant takes on a rich smoky flavor when grilled over a fire—it's just not the same when you broil it indoors.

vegetable oil for brushing grill
1 Japanese eggplant, thinly sliced
3 tablespoons bottled Caesar salad dressing
8 slices (3/4-inch thick) crusty, firm country-style
  Italian bread
2 garlic cloves, peeled and halved lengthwise
olive oil
1 cup jarred olive salad
8 large basil leaves, torn or shredded

• Prepare a grill for barbecuing and brush grill rack with oil. Place eggplant slices on a foil-lined baking sheet. Brush on both sides with dressing. Grill over medium-high heat until tender and browned, turning once, about 3 minutes per side. Place on a cutting board and cut into bite-size pieces.

• Grill bread slices on both sides. Rub garlic on one side of the slices and brush with olive oil. Top with eggplant slices, olive salad, and sprinkle with basil.

PER SERVING: 193 CALORIES; 3 G PROTEIN; 17 G CARBOHYDRATES;
13 G TOTAL FAT; 2 G SATURATED FAT; 0 MG CHOLESTEROL; 493 MG SODIUM

PREP TIME: 15 MINUTES   COOKING TIME: 15 MINUTES

Grilled Summer Squash Crostini

MAKES 4 SERVINGS

Here the plain flavors of zucchini and yellow squash are concentrated by grilling and are heightened by spicy arugula and salty curls of fresh Parmigiano Reggiano cheese.

1 small zucchini, thinly sliced
1 small yellow summer squash, thinly sliced
bottled Caesar or citrus salad dressing for brushing
4 slices crusty Italian bread
8 to 12 leaves cleaned arugula
shavings of Parmigiano Reggiano cheese for serving
fresh oregano for serving

• Preheat broiler. Line baking sheet with foil; arrange zucchini and squash slices in a single layer on top and brush with dressing. Broil 4 inches from heat source until golden brown, 8 to 10 minutes, turning after 4 to 5 minutes and brushing with dressing after turning. Grill bread slices on both sides after grilling squashes.

• Arrange arugula on toasts; brush with dressing. Top with alternating slices of both kinds of squash, the cheese, and then bits of oregano.

PER SERVING: 125 CALORIES; 5 G PROTEIN; 17 G CARBOHYDRATES; 4 G TOTAL
FAT; 1 G SATURATED FAT; 4 MG CHOLESTEROL; 281 MG SODIUM

COOKS' TIP:

If you can't find arugula, you can use watercress leaves.

PREP TIME: 10 MINUTES   COOKING TIME: 2 MINUTES

Grilled Spicy Pita Wedges

MAKES 6 SERVINGS

These are great little crackers, either used for dips or plain, on their own.

1/4 cup bottled Italian salad dressing
1/2 teaspoon hot paprika or chili powder, or more
  to taste
6 pita breads, with pockets or without

• Prepare a grill for barbecue. Mix dressing and paprika in a glass measuring cup. Lightly brush pitas on both sides with dressing mixture and grill over medium-high heat about 2 minutes, turning every 30 seconds. Stack pitas on a cutting board; cut in half. Stack halves; cut stack into desired-size triangles.

PER SERVING: 123 CALORIES; 3 G PROTEIN; 17 G CARBOHYDRATES;
5 G TOTAL FAT; 0.7 G SATURATED FAT; 0 MG CHOLESTEROL; 227 MG SODIUM

COOKS' TIP:

You can use corn or flour tortillas or flour wraps instead of the pitas. Cut them into triangles with a pizza wheel for serving.

PREP TIME: 20 MINUTES   COOKING TIME: 10 MINUTES

Almond and Artichoke Bruschetta

MAKES 16 BRUSCHETTA

These appetizers are delicious without the prosciutto di Parma, but using it will make each bite memorable.

1/2 cup slivered, blanched almonds
1 jar (6.5 ounces) marinated artichoke hearts
16 slices (1/2-inch thick) French baguette
2 large garlic cloves, halved
16 thin slices of prosciutto di Parma, halved
  horizontally

• Prepare a grill for barbecue. Toast the almonds in a wire mesh pouch on the grill over medium coals or in a nonstick skillet over medium heat 3 to 5 minutes, turning or stirring, until fragrant and lightly browned. Let cool, then finely chop.

• Drain the artichoke hearts, reserving the oil, and coarsely chop. Over indirect heat, toast the bread slices on both sides. Scrape the garlic over one side of each toast and brush with the artichoke oil. Loosely fold a piece of prosciutto onto each toast. Top with some artichokes and sprinkle with almonds. Arrange the bruschetta on a platter and serve.

PER SERVING: 134 CALORIES; 5 G PROTEIN; 18 G CARBOHYDRATES;
5 G TOTAL FAT; 0.7 G SATURATED FAT; 4 MG CHOLESTEROL; 289 MG SODIUM

COOKS' TIP:

You can use chopped smoked almonds if you have them on hand instead of searching for the slivered plain nuts.

PREP TIME: 15 MINUTES   COOKING TIME: 12 MINUTES

Grilled Corn and Black Bean Bruschetta

MAKES 6 SERVINGS

Fire-roasted corn mixed with colorful components makes one of the tastiest, easiest, and most dramatic appetizers you may ever serve!

2 ears of corn, husks and silks removed

1 tablespoon extra virgin olive oil

1 cup canned black beans, rinsed and drained

1/2 cup fresh or jarred chunky salsa

1/4 cup chopped cilantro

salt and freshly ground pepper to taste

12 slices (3/4-inch thick) crusty, firm country-style Italian bread

2 large garlic cloves, peeled and halved lengthwise

• Prepare grill for a barbecue. Brush corn ears with oil and cook over medium-hot to hot coals until charred and cooked, 5 to 7 minutes, turning every 1 to 2 minutes. Remove to a cutting board and when they are cool enough to handle, cut kernels from the cobs with a sharp knife, scraping the cobs of their juices. Scrape corn and juices into a large bowl and add beans, salsa, cilantro, salt, and pepper. Toss gently.

• Grill bread on both sides. Rub garlic on one side of bread and brush with olive oil. Top with corn mixture.

PER SERVING: 122 CALORIES; 5 G PROTEIN; 20.5 G CARBOHYDRATES; 3 G TOTAL FAT; 0.3 G SATURATED FAT; 0 MG CHOLESTEROL; 291 MG SODIUM

COOKS' TIP:

You can use canned small red beans or soak and cook some dried Jacob's Cattle beans instead of using the black beans.

PREP TIME: 20 MINUTES   COOKING TIME: 20 MINUTES

Grilled Salsa Quesadillas

MAKES 6 SERVINGS

These are great for a crowd because the quesadillas cook quickly and are substantially cheesy enough to satisfy that wave of cocktail-hour hunger.

8 *plain or flavored (tomato or jalapeño) flour tortilla wraps (6 inches in diameter)*
nonstick cooking spray
1/2 cup prepared salsa (mild, medium, or hot)
2 cups shredded cheddar cheese or other hard cheese
1/2 cup finely snipped chives, thinly sliced scallions, or minced red onions

COOKS' TIP:

You can use 4 flour wraps (12 inches in diameter) of any flavor instead of the smaller tortillas.

- Prepare a grill for barbecuing. Spray one side of 4 wraps with cooking spray and place them, sprayed side down, on a sheet of plastic wrap. Spread one-fourth of the salsa over each sprayed wrap and sprinkle with one-fourth of the cheese and one-fourth of the chives. Top each with a remaining wrap. Place on a baking sheet and repeat with remaining ingredients.

- Spray top of quesadillas with cooking spray and grill 2 or 3 at a time 3 minutes or until cheese starts to melt.

- Flip quesadillas over using a wide spatula. Grill 2 or 3 minutes, until cheese is nicely melted, and slide quesadillas onto cutting board. Using a pizza cutter, cut into wedges or rough 2-inch pieces.

PER SERVING: 282 CALORIES; 13 G PROTEIN; 23 G CARBOHYDRATES; 15 G TOTAL FAT; 9 G SATURATED FAT; 40 MG CHOLESTEROL; 507 MG SODIUM

PREP TIME: 15 MINUTES   COOKING TIME: 35 MINUTES

Margarita-Glazed Chicken Wings

MAKES 12 SERVINGS

The components of summer's favorite drink make a tasty glaze for the wings. Since margarita mix contains a lot of sugar, be sure to watch the chicken carefully to make sure the skin doesn't burn. Turn the pieces frequently and move them to a cooler spot on the grill to cook through once the skin has crisped.

nonstick cooking spray

4 1/2 pounds precut chicken wings (only the first 2 joints, separated, without tips)

kosher salt and freshly ground pepper

1 cup bottled margarita mix

1/2 cup tequila

1 teaspoon chili powder

1/4 cup fresh lime juice

lime wedges for garnish

COOKS' TIP:

The glaze is tasty for baby back pork ribs, too. You will have to blanch them a minute in boiling water before grilling so they will cook more quickly.

• Prepare an outdoor grill for barbecue. Preheat the oven to 500° F. Line 2 large rimmed baking sheets with foil and grease with cooking spray. Spread out the wing pieces on the baking sheets; season with salt and pepper. Bake for 10 minutes, turn pieces over and cook 10 minutes longer, or until the wings are almost cooked through and lightly browned.

• While wings cook, combine the margarita mix, tequila, and chili powder in a small saucepan and heat to boiling over medium-high heat. Boil, stirring occasionally, until the glaze is reduced to 1 cup, about 5 minutes. Stir in the lime juice. Pour half the glaze into a large bowl and half into a small pitcher.

• Place the wing pieces into the bowl and toss with the glaze. Grill the wing pieces over medium-high heat on both sides until skin is crisped and meat is cooked through, about 15 minutes, turning once. Transfer to a platter and sprinkle lightly with salt. Garnish with lime wedges. Serve hot or at room temperature with the remaining glaze.

PER SERVING (ABOUT 4 WING HALVES EACH): 360 CALORIES; 31 G PROTEIN; 3 G CARBOHYDRATES; 22 G TOTAL FAT; 6 G SATURATED FAT; 95 MG CHOLESTEROL; 94 MG SODIUM

PREP TIME: 10 MINUTES   COOKING TIME: 10 MINUTES

Grilled Scallions with Tomato and Smoked-Almond Sauce

MAKES 8 SERVINGS WITH ABOUT 2 CUPS SAUCE

This Spanish appetizer usually calls for thin spring onions, but since scallions are so easy to get and are delicious grilled, that's what is called for here. The classic sauce, known as Romesco, can be adapted to what you have on hand: try some homemade or jarred roasted red peppers instead of the tomatoes, and sambal oelek or other chili sauce instead of the chipotle chile in adobo sauce.

oil for brushing
3 bunches scallions, trimmed and rinsed
kosher or sea salt

SAUCE
1/2 cup smoked almonds (prepared or homemade)
1 1/2 cups canned diced tomatoes with roasted garlic
   and some juice
2 tablespoons red-wine vinegar, or more to taste
1 teaspoon chipotle chile in adobo sauce, or more
   to taste
salt and freshly ground pepper

• Prepare a grill for barbecuing. Oil the grill rack. Place the scallions on a foil-lined baking sheet and brush with oil. Place scallions on the grill rack perpendicular to the grill rungs so they won't fall through. Grill over hot heat, turning with tongs and sprinkling with salt, until charred and tender, 8 to 10 minutes. Remove to a paper-towel lined baking sheet; roll up scallions in the paper towel and set aside 10 to 15 minutes.

• Grind almonds in food processor until evenly cut up but not enough to start forming a paste. Add the tomatoes, vinegar, and chipotle chili; process until puréed, adding only enough extra juice from the tomatoes to make a thick coating sauce. Taste and adjust seasoning, adding salt only if needed.

• To serve, remove charred outer layers of scallions. Serve whole with the sauce for dipping.

GRILLED SCALLIONS, PER SERVING: 32 CALORIES; 1 G PROTEIN;
4 G CARBOHYDRATES; 2 G TOTAL FAT; 0 G SATURATED FAT;
0 MG CHOLESTEROL; 152 MG SODIUM
TOMATO AND SMOKED-ALMOND SAUCE, PER SERVING: 67 CALORIES;
3 G PROTEIN; 3 G CARBOHYDRATES; 5 G TOTAL FAT; 0 G SATURATED FAT;
0 MG CHOLESTEROL; 112 MG SODIUM

COOKS' TIP:

The grilled scallions are delicious sprinkled with fine sea salt if you don't have time to make the sauce.

Grilled Escarole and Bean Salad

MAKES 4 SERVINGS

Even though escarole is considered a bitter-tasting green, it is sweetened somewhat by slightly caramelizing it over the coals. Most prepared dressings and 3-bean salads contain a pinch of sugar, so they, too, are added as a counterbalance.

vegetable oil for brushing grill

1 head escarole, quartered through the core

3 tablespoons bottled garlic vinaigrette dressing

8 slices (3/4-inch thick) crusty, firm country-style
   Italian bread

2 garlic cloves, peeled and halved lengthwise

olive oil

2 cups marinated 3-bean salad

1/4 cup torn or shredded flat-leaf parsley

• Prepare a grill for barbecuing and brush grill rack with oil. Place escarole wedges on a foil-lined baking sheet. Brush with dressing. Grill over medium-high heat until tender and browned, turning once, about 4 minutes in all. Place on plates.

• Grill bread slices on both sides. Rub garlic on one side of the slices and brush with olive oil. Top escarole with bean salad and sprinkle with the parsley. Serve with garlic toasts.

PER SERVING: 221 CALORIES; 4 G PROTEIN; 31 G CARBOHYDRATES; 10 G TOTAL FAT; 1 G SATURATED FAT; 0 MG CHOLESTEROL; 267 MG SODIUM

COOKS' TIP:

If you can't find escarole, you can grill some of the dark outer leaves of a head of Romaine lettuce.

PREP TIME: 10 MINUTES   COOKING TIME: 1 MINUTE

Prosciutto di Parma and Garlic Cheese Breadsticks

MAKES 24 BREADSTICKS

There are endless variations to this concept, including using packaged dried beef instead of the tasty ham. Another simple combination is dipping the "top" end of the breadstick in honey, draining it, and wrapping the ham around the honey end and down the breadstick like a bandage.

6 thin (but thicker than paper-thin) slices prosciutto di Parma or other tasty ham
1 package (5.2 ounces) herb-and-garlic soft cheese, at room temperature
24 crisp Italian breadsticks

• Spread out the prosciutto slices on cutting board. Using a pizza cutter, cut prosciutto in half crosswise and lengthwise.

• Spoon 1 teaspoon cheese onto the middle of one end of each prosciutto strip. Top with a breadstick. Roll up from cheese end spiral-fashion; grill over a medium-hot fire until cheese starts to melt, about 1 minute.

PER BREADSTICK: 45 CALORIES; 1 G PROTEIN; 4 G CARBOHYDRATES; 3 G TOTAL FAT; 2 G SATURATED FAT; 7 MG CHOLESTEROL; 96 MG SODIUM

COOKS' TIP:
The breadsticks will stay crisper if you grill and serve them right after wrapping.

PREP TIME: 15 MINUTES   COOKING TIME: 6 MINUTES

Grilled Rosemary-Lamb Cocktail Meatballs

MAKES 8 APPETIZER SERVINGS

Rosemary sprigs are strong and moist enough to make skewers for foods that require short-term grilling. Here the stripped-off leaves are added to the lamb, so the intact little ends of the sprigs give diners visual and aromatic notice of the flavor that lies ahead.

8 sprigs (6 inches each) fresh rosemary

1 pound ground lamb

2 large eggs

1/3 cup Italian-seasoned dry bread crumbs

3/8 cup bottled citrus salad dressing

1 cup Greek-style plain yogurt

2 tablespoons grated onion

salt and freshly ground pepper

- Prepare a grill for barbecue. Remove the rosemary leaves from the stems, leaving the small leaves at the tip intact. Set the stems aside. Finely chop enough rosemary leaves to measure 1 tablespoon. Freeze the remaining leaves for another use.

- In a large bowl, combine the chopped rosemary, lamb, eggs, bread crumbs, and 1/4 cup dressing. Mix with your hands until combined. Form the mixture into 32 meatballs and press the balls around the stripped portion of the rosemary sprigs, with 4 balls on each sprig. Place on a baking sheet and brush with 2 tablespoons dressing.

- Mix yogurt with remaining 2 tablespoons dressing and the onion, and season with salt and pepper. Set aside.

- Grill meatballs over a hot fire for 6 minutes, turning every minute, until firm, cooked through, and browned. Serve with the yogurt mixture.

PER SERVING: 213 CALORIES; 14 G PROTEIN; 7 G CARBOHYDRATES;
14 G TOTAL FAT; 5 G SATURATED FAT; 93 MG CHOLESTEROL; 115 MG SODIUM

COOKS' TIP:

Alternate small squares of red, green, and yellow bell peppers between the meatballs.

PREP TIME: 30 MINUTES   COOKING TIME: 6 MINUTES

Spicy Tofu Kebabs

MAKES 4 SERVINGS

Pickle juice is great for grilling. It is an all-in-one marinade and basting sauce and contains a tasty balance of seasonings and a little sugar to make a nice caramelizing glaze.

1 pound firm tofu, cut into 16 one-inch chunks
1 red jalapeño chile, seeded and minced
1/4 cup sweet pickle juice
2 tablespoons white miso
2 tablespoons hot water
1 tablespoon grapeseed oil
1 teaspoon nigella seeds (optional)
1 teaspoon sesame seeds
12 Chinese pea pods, stem and strings removed,
    halved crosswise

• Prepare grill for barbecue. Soak four bamboo or wood skewers in hot water. Place tofu in bowl and place a loaf pan on top. Weight with two 1-pound cans and let stand for 20 minutes. Drain off liquid and cut tofu into 3/4-inch cubes.

• Whisk jalapeño, pickle juice, miso, water, oil, nigella seeds, if using, and sesame seeds in a large bowl until blended. Add tofu and gently toss to coat. Thread tofu onto skewers, alternating with Chinese peapods.

• Place skewers on grill rack over medium-hot coals or on rack in broiler pan 6 inches from heat source. Grill, covered if possible, or broil until heated through, turning every 2 minutes, about 6 minutes in all.

PER SERVING: 127 CALORIES; 11 G PROTEIN; 10 G CARBOHYDRATES;
6 G TOTAL FAT; 1 G SATURATED FAT; 0 MG CHOLESTEROL; 417 MG SODIUM

COOKS' TIP:

If you can't find nigella seeds, use black sesame seeds or chopped chives.

PREP TIME: 30 MINUTES   COOKING TIME: 16 MINUTES

Roasted-Corn and Polenta Tamales in Fresh Corn Husks

MAKES 8 SERVINGS

"Reassembling" the ears of corn with a double corn filling adds excitement to grilled corn.

2 *ears of corn on the cob*
2 *tablespoons corn oil, plus extra for the grill*
8 *slices (1-inch thick) of polenta from*
  a 19 ounce tube
2 *tablespoons water*
1 *link chorizo, spicy or plain (6 ounces)*
1 *cup diced Monterey Jack cheese, plain or*
  with jalapeños
1/4 *cup chopped scallions*
2 *tablespoons chopped fresh cilantro*
salt and pepper to taste
1/2 *cup Mexican or other sour cream for serving*
1/2 *cup salsa for serving*

● Prepare grill for barbecuing. Carefully remove the husks and silk from the ears of corn, cutting around the stem end of the corn if necessary to release the inner husks. Arrange the outer thick husks in one pile and the inner ones in another pile. Set aside.

● Brush corn ears with oil and cook over medium-hot to hot coals until charred and cooked, 5 to 7 minutes, turning every 1 to 2 minutes. Remove to a cutting board and let cool. Meanwhile, break up polenta into 1-inch pieces and place in a microwave-safe bowl.

Sprinkle with the water. Remove casing from chorizo and chop into 1/4-inch dice. Add to polenta. Cover with plastic wrap; heat in microwave on HIGH power 3 minutes, stirring every minute, until evenly smooth. Set aside.

● When corn ears are cool enough to handle, cut from the cobs with a sharp knife or cleaver and add to polenta mixture. Scrape the cobs of their juices and add to the polenta mixture. Add cheese, scallions, cilantro, salt, and pepper to polenta mixture.

● For each tamale, spread out 2 outer husks flat on the work surface, overlapping sides slightly and wide ends by 3 inches. Weight down ends with a table knife. Repeat to make 8 husk pairs in all. Spoon one-eighth of the polenta mixture lengthwise over center of each wide portion and cover each with two inner husks. Fold ends of outer husks around inner husks and tie ends with kitchen string. Place on a foil-lined baking sheet and brush on all sides with oil.

● Brush the grill rack with oil and grill tamales, outer husk side down, over medium-high heat 4 minutes. Turn tamales over and grill until heated through, about 2 more minutes. Serve with sour cream and salsa.

PER SERVING: 315 CALORIES; 13 G PROTEIN; 25 G CARBOHYDRATES; 19 G TOTAL FAT; 8 G SATURATED FAT; 37 MG CHOLESTEROL; 803 MG SODIUM

PREP TIME: 12 MINUTES   COOKING TIME: 12 MINUTES

Pepper-Cheese Stuffed Onions

MAKES 6 SERVINGS

You can top the onions with the cheese mixture and place on a double-thickness of foil, folding up the edges to make a package, and refrigerate up to a day ahead of cooking. Cook the onions in the packet on the grill until the cheese melts.

6 sweet onions (Vidalia, Texas Sweet, Walla-Walla, or Maui) (5 ounces each)
1 package (5.2 ounces) soft cheese flavored with peppercorns, at room temperature
2 tablespoons Italian-seasoned dry bread crumbs
2 tablespoons extra virgin olive oil plus extra for brushing the grill pan

COOKS' TIP:

To turn these onions into a hearty first course, you can scoop out the center layers of the onions and stir in about 1 cup cooked ground beef or chicken to the cheese mixture. Grill them on the grill or in a packet; place any leftover whole onions on a microwave-safe plate and cook them for about 2 minutes on HIGH power for a satisfying lunch.

● Prepare a grill for barbecuing. Soak 24 wooden or bamboo skewers in hot water. Heat a 3-quart saucepan of salted water to boiling.

● Peel onions and cut off the top third of each for another use. Skewer each of the onions crosswise with 4 wooden toothpicks, each poked in crosswise and parallel (positioned at twelve and six o'clock and three and nine o'clock).

● Heat a 3-quart saucepan of salted water to boiling and add the onions. Boil onions 6 minutes and carefully remove with tongs to a colander. Let stand 5 minutes and rinse with gently flowing cold water.

● In a medium bowl, mix the cheese, bread crumbs, and 2 tablespoons olive oil. Spoon the filling on top of cut sides of onions. Place a vegetable grill pan on the hot grill and brush with olive oil. Place the onions in the grill pan and cover the grill. Cook the onions until evenly charred on the outside and the filling is hot, about 6 minutes, checking the onions after 4 minutes and moving them to a cooler part of the grill if necessary to keep the bottoms from burning before the filling is hot.

PER SERVING: 204 CALORIES; 4 G PROTEIN; 14 G CARBOHYDRATES; 16 G TOTAL FAT; 8 G SATURATED FAT; 29 MG CHOLESTEROL; 191 MG SODIUM

PREP TIME: 20 MINUTES   COOKING TIME: 7 MINUTES

Sausage on Lemongrass Skewers

MAKES 6 SERVINGS

Grilling over coals brings out the best in a sausage and so does grilling on stalks of tangy, fragrant lemongrass. Bits of the inside tender portion of the stalks are mixed in with the sausage and add a citrusy accent, like a drop or two of fresh lemon juice.

8 fat stalks fresh lemongrass
2 pounds sausage (pork, duck, venison, chicken,
    turkey, or seafood) with some fruit or dried tomato
    added, removed from the casings
vegetable oil for brushing
salt and freshly ground pepper
chopped peanuts
lime wedges for serving

COOKS' TIP:

You can find lemongrass in Asian grocery stores. The stalks freeze well for future grilling.

- Prepare a grill for barbecuing. Cut off the root ends and top two-thirds of the lemongrass stalks. Remove and discard the first 2 outer layers of all the pieces. Cut the top portions into 5-inch lengths. Mince the tender bottom third of the bulbs and place one-fourth of the minced bulbs into a large bowl. Freeze the remainder for another use.

- Mix the sausage with the minced lemongrass bulbs in a bowl. Divide into 16 equal portions with wet hands and mold each around a length of lemongrass stalk, leaving about 1 inch of the ends clear. Place lemongrass "skewers" on a foil-lined baking sheet and brush with oil. Sprinkle lightly with salt and pepper.

- Grill the skewers over medium-high heat, turning to cook on all sides, about 7 minutes in all. Remove to a platter and sprinkle with peanuts. Serve with lime wedges.

PER SERVING: 372 CALORIES; 17 G PROTEIN; 2 G CARBOHYDRATES; 32 G TOTAL FAT; 10 G SATURATED FAT; 75 MG CHOLESTEROL; 1,174 MG SODIUM

PREP TIME: 10 MINUTES COOKING TIME: 1 MINUTE

Tomato and Mozzarella Kebabs

MAKES 6 SERVINGS

Part-skim-milk mozzarella melts more slowly than the whole-milk variety, so if you're using the latter, such as the pre-marinated little cheese balls called bocconcini, be sure to heat them over a lower fire and watch them carefully.

1/4 cup Italian dressing
1/2 teaspoon crushed red pepper flakes
8 ounces fresh mozzarella, cut into 3/4-inch cubes
2 pints cherry tomatoes (a mix of red and yellow)
1/4 cup torn fresh basil leaves

● Prepare a grill for barbecue. Combine the dressing and pepper flakes in a shallow bowl and mix well. Add the mozzarella and tomatoes and toss to coat. Thread pieces of mozzarella and the tomatoes onto 6 skewers, placing 2 tomatoes together between the chunks of cheese and alternating the colors of the tomatoes. Grill skewers over a hot fire until cheese is lightly browned and starting to melt, about 1 minute, turning every 30 seconds. Slide the cheese and tomatoes onto plates and sprinkle with basil.

PER SERVING: 173 CALORIES; 8 G PROTEIN; 7 G CARBOHYDRATES; 13 G TOTAL FAT; 6 G SATURATED FAT; 30 MG CHOLESTEROL; 227 MG SODIUM

COOKS' TIP:

Cubes of feta or provolone melt more slowly than other cheeses, so they grill nicely alongside the tomatoes.

PREP TIME: 5 MINUTES   COOKING TIME: 2 MINUTES

Roasted-Garlic and Parsley Bread

MAKES 10 SERVINGS

The sweet aroma and creamy texture of roasted garlic as it gushes from each clove excites the crowd.

1 thin baguette
6 tablespoons unsalted butter
8 cloves roasted garlic (recipe, page 165)
salt and freshly ground pepper
1 cup torn flat-leaf parsley leaves

● Prepare a grill for barbecuing. Cut the baguette in half along its length. Grill the bread slices over medium-hot heat, cut side down, until browned and crisped, about 2 minutes.

● Melt the butter in a small bowl in the microwave and squeeze the garlic from the cloves into the butter. Mix well. Brush the mixture over the cut sides of the bread and sprinkle with salt and pepper and then the parsley. Cut breads crosswise into 2-inch pieces.

PER SERVING: 145 CALORIES; 3 G PROTEIN; 16 G CARBOHYDRATES; 8 G TOTAL FAT; 5 G SATURATED FAT; 19 MG CHOLESTEROL; 293 MG SODIUM

COOKS' TIP:

You can use extra virgin olive oil in place of some of the butter for a different flavor.

PREP TIME: 15 MINUTES   COOKING TIME: 8 MINUTES

Cheesy Pull-Apart Bread

MAKES 12 SERVINGS

Your family and friends will have fun tearing into this finger-licking loaf. The pieces are small enough for everyone to have a taste as the bread comes off the fire.

1 package (5.2 ounces) garlic-and-herb soft cheese
*   spread, at room temperature*
1 stick unsalted butter, softened
1 loaf Italian bread (1 pound)

● Prepare a grill for barbecuing. Mix cheese spread and butter in a bowl until blended.

● With a serrated knife, slice bread diagonally almost all the way through 12 times at 1½-inch intervals. Spread half the cheese mixture on cut sides. Turn bread loaf so that the ends are reversed and slice the loaf diagonally almost all the way through 12 times to make diamond-shape pieces. Spread remaining cheese mixture on newly cut sides of bread.

● Wrap bread in heavy-duty aluminum foil and place loaf, top side up, on grill rack to the side of medium-hot coals. Heat bread on covered grill 8 minutes, or until the bread is hot and the cheese is melted.

PER SERVING: 230 CALORIES; 4 G PROTEIN; 19 G CARBOHYDRATES; 12 G TOTAL FAT; 9 G SATURATED FAT; 39 MG CHOLESTEROL; 312 MG SODIUM

PREP TIME: 10 MINUTES   COOKING TIME: 14 MINUTES

Olive and Almond Flat Breads

MAKE 12 SERVINGS

There are countless ways to enjoy these savory hors d'oeuvres. Pair the flat breads with other mild cow's-milk cheeses, such as Fontina, Camembert, or rind-less Brie. Roasted peppers, sun-dried tomatoes, caramelized onions,

or anchovies could be substituted for any of the top-pings.

4 flat breads (6 or 7 inches in diameter) or pocketless pita breads

extra virgin olive oil, preferably Spanish, for brushing

1 1/4 pounds Manchego or other mild cheese from cow's milk, such as Italian Fontina or Taleggio, sliced thinly with a cheese plane

1/4 cup Spanish green olives, pitted and chopped

1/4 cup chopped salted and roasted almonds

● Prepare a grill for barbecuing. Place the flat breads on a foil-lined baking sheet and brush lightly on both sides with olive oil. Toast them directly on the grill rack for 6 minutes, or until golden. Remove to foil-lined baking sheet.

● Spread the cheese on the breads, leaving a 1-inch border all around. Sprinkle with the olives and almonds. Grill the breads, cheese side up, to one side of medium-hot coals with the grill covered until the cheese melts, about 8 minutes. Cut each bread into 4 wedges.

PER SERVING: 275 CALORIES; 14 G PROTEIN; 11 G CARBOHYDRATES; 19 G TOTAL FAT; 10 G SATURATED FAT; 55 MG CHOLESTEROL; 372 MG SODIUM

Sweet and Sour Cocktail Onions

MAKES 4 SERVINGS

Aleppo pepper comes from Turkey and eastern Syria and pomegranate molasses is used on grilled meats in eastern Turkey and Central Asia. Both products can be found in Middle Eastern grocery stores.

1 tablespoon olive oil, plus extra for the grill

1 tablespoon pomegranate molasses, or regular unsulfured molasses, or pure maple syrup

24 pickled cocktail onions, drained and rinsed with hot water

aleppo pepper or hot smoked paprika or chili powder for sprinkling

- Prepare a grill for barbecuing. Soak four bamboo or wooden skewers in water. Grease a grill rack.

- Mix oil and molasses in a small bowl and add onions; toss to coat. Thread onions on skewers. Grill, turning skewers and basting with oil and molasses mixture, until onions are hot and coating is caramelized, about 3 minutes. Sprinkle with pepper and slide onto plates. Serve hot.

PER SERVING: 53 CALORIES; 0 G PROTEIN; 6 G CARBOHYDRATES; 4 G TOTAL FAT; 0 G SATURATED FAT; 0 MG CHOLESTEROL; 28 MG SODIUM

COOKS' TIP:

Be sure to pat the onions dry with paper towels before adding them to the molasses mixture. That way the coating will stick to the onions enough to make a nice glaze.

PREP TIME: 5 MINUTES   COOKING TIME: 1 MINUTE

Grilled Pita for Sandwiches

MAKES 6 SERVINGS

Pita is usually warmed on a grill in the Middle East just before eating or filling. A few seconds over hot coals quickly adds a fresh-baked flavor to the bread.

6 pita breads with pockets
1 tablespoon olive oil

• Prepare a grill for barbecue. Cut off "top" third of pitas. (Save to slice into triangles and use for dipping into hummus or baba ganouche.) Lightly brush pitas with olive oil and grill over medium-high heat for about 30 seconds; turn and grill just until heated through but not crisp, about 1 minute in all.

PER SERVING: 98 CALORIES; 3 G PROTEIN; 16 G CARBOHYDRATES; 3 G TOTAL FAT; 0 G SATURATED FAT; 0 MG CHOLESTEROL; 150 MG SODIUM

PREP TIME: 10 MINUTES   COOKING TIME: 2 MINUTES

Garlic-Tomato Bread

MAKES 10 SERVINGS

This combination of simple ingredients is enjoyed whenever fresh vine-ripened tomatoes and fruity olive oil are at hand.

1 thin baguette
2 large garlic cloves, peeled and halved lengthwise
4 ripe plum tomatoes, halved lengthwise and seeds removed with your thumb
1/3 cup Spanish or other fruity extra virgin olive oil
sea salt
freshly ground pepper

• Prepare a grill for barbecuing. Cut the baguette in half along its length. Grill the bread slices over medium-hot heat, cut side down, until browned and crisped, about 2 minutes.

• Rub the cut sides of the garlic over the cut sides of the bread halves. Rub cut sides of tomatoes over the cut sides of the bread. Drizzle the toasts with olive oil and sprinkle with salt and pepper. Cut breads crosswise into 2-inch pieces.

PER SERVING: 150 CALORIES; 3 G PROTEIN; 16 G CARBOHYDRATES; 8 G TOTAL FAT; 5 G SATURATED FAT; 0 MG CHOLESTEROL; 291 MG SODIUM

Salads

Grilled Curried-Chicken Salad •

Grilled Paprika Chicken and •
Vegetable Salad

Thai Beef Salad •

Grilled Cucumber Salad •

Leek and Potato Salad with •
Spicy Buttermilk Dressing

Warm Salmon Salad with •
Yuzu Vinaigrette

• Grilled Fruit Salad

• Shrimp Salad with
Green Goddess Dressing

• Grilled Waldorf Salad with Mint

• Deconstructed Salad Niçoise

• Warm Pasta Salad with Lemon Chicken
and Mushrooms

• Ham and Pineapple Salad with
Sweet and Spicy Ginger Dressing

Grilled Curried-Chicken Salad

MAKES 4 SERVINGS

You can use catfish fillets or boneless pork chops instead of chicken and serve them on a bed of the slaw.

1 tablespoon vegetable oil plus extra for the grill

4 skinless, boneless chicken cutlets (8 ounces each)

3 teaspoons curry powder

1/2 teaspoon celery salt (optional)

3/4 cup lemon-flavored or plain yogurt, preferably Greek style

2 tablespoons fresh lemon juice

salt and freshly ground pepper to taste

1 bag coleslaw mix (10 ounces), cabbage and carrots

2 scallions, trimmed and finely chopped

1/2 cup trail mix (without chocolate chips!)

- Prepare a grill for barbecuing. Oil the rack. Brush chicken pieces on both sides with oil. Mix 2 teaspoons curry powder with celery salt, if using, or 1/2 teaspoon plain salt and 1/4 teaspoon pepper, and rub over chicken. Grill chicken over a medium-hot fire, turning with tongs several times, until cooked through, about 8 minutes in all. Transfer to a cutting board and let stand 5 minutes.

- Meanwhile, mix yogurt, lemon juice, remaining 1 teaspoon curry powder and salt and pepper to taste. Add coleslaw mix, scallions, and trail mix and toss to coat. Slice chicken into 3/4-inch pieces and add to slaw mixture. Toss to mix.

PER SERVING: 278 CALORIES; 31 G PROTEIN; 17 G CARBOHYDRATES; 10 G TOTAL FAT; 2 G SATURATED FAT; 70 MG CHOLESTEROL; 309 MG SODIUM

COOKS' TIP:

Use a freshly opened container of curry powder for the best flavor.

Grilled Paprika Chicken and Vegetable Salad

MAKES 4 SERVINGS

Smoked paprika is a standard ingredient in Spanish kitchens and comes in hot, bittersweet, and mild variations. You can smell them and get a sense of their flavor intensity.

4 tablespoons extra virgin olive oil plus extra for
   the grill
4 chicken cutlets (6 ounces each)
2 red bell peppers, very thinly sliced
1 medium onion, very thinly sliced
2 garlic cloves, crushed through a press
1 1/2 teaspoons thyme leaves
1 teaspoon kosher salt, or more to taste
1 teaspoon hot smoked Spanish paprika or other
   hot paprika, or more to taste
1 small head frisée, torn into bite-size pieces
1 tablespoon sherry vinegar
2 tablespoons finely chopped flat-leaf parsley

● Prepare a grill for barbecuing. Oil a vegetable grilling pan and set on the grill to preheat. Place the chicken and vegetables on a foil-lined baking sheet. Mix 4 tablespoons oil, the garlic, thyme, 1 teaspoon salt, and 1 teaspoon paprika together in a cup and drizzle over the chicken and vegetables. Toss to mix. Place vegetables in the preheated grill pan and cook over medium-high heat until crisp-tender. Remove to a bowl and taste.

● Oil the grill rack and grill the chicken until cooked through, about 4 minutes on each side. Transfer the chicken to a cutting board and slice crosswise into 1/2-inch wide strips.

● Add the frisée and vinegar to the bell pepper mixture, season to taste with salt and paprika, and toss to mix. Mound the salad on plates and top with sliced chicken. Sprinkle with parsley and serve.

PER SERVING: 307 CALORIES; 30 G PROTEIN; 12 G CARBOHYDRATES;
16 G TOTAL FAT; 2 G SATURATED FAT; 68 MG CHOLESTEROL; 109 MG SODIUM

COOKS' TIP:

You can sprinkle some sliced pimiento-stuffed or sliced pitted Manzanilla olives over the finished dish for extra flavor and color.

Thai Beef Salad

MAKES 6 SERVINGS

Everyone has a favorite version of this salad but this recipe is special because the beef is grilled over flavorful coals.

2 tablespoons grapeseed or canola oil, plus extra for
   the grill

1 sirloin steak or top round, about 1 1/4-inches thick
   (about 8 ounces)

3 garlic cloves, crushed through a press

salt and freshly ground pepper

1/4 cup plus 2 tablespoons fresh lime juice

3 tablespoons Asian fish sauce

1/4 cup warm water

2 Thai chiles, minced

1 tablespoon sugar

5 small scallions, cut into 1-inch lengths

1 medium tomato, halved lengthwise and thickly
   sliced

1 Kirby cucumber, thinly sliced

1 cup cilantro leaves

1/2 cup torn mint leaves

1/2 cup chopped peanuts

● Prepare a grill for barbecuing. Oil the grill rack. Place the beef on a foil-lined baking sheet, brush on both sides with 2 tablespoons oil. Rub with garlic, and sprinkle with salt and pepper. Grill the steak over medium-high heat for 4 to 6 minutes on each side for medium rare. Remove to a cutting board and let stand at least 10 minutes. Thinly slice the steak.

● In a large bowl, mix the lime juice, fish sauce, water, chiles, and sugar; stir to dissolve the sugar. Add the beef, scallions, tomato, cucumber, cilantro, and mint; toss gently to mix. Sprinkle with peanuts and serve.

PER SERVING: 390 CALORIES; 26 G PROTEIN; 10 G CARBOHYDRATES; 28 G TOTAL FAT; 8 G SATURATED FAT; 76 MG CHOLESTEROL; 964 MG SODIUM

COOKS' TIP:

Using thin scallions will make each bite a balanced mix of flavors. If you can find only fat ones, thinly slice them crosswise into rounds.

PREP TIME: 10 MINUTES   COOKING TIME: 5 MINUTES

Grilled Cucumber Salad

MAKES 6 SERVINGS

You can use 1/4 cup bottled salad dressing with lime instead of making the dressing from scratch.

vegetable oil

1 European cucumber

12 fat scallions, trimmed and cut into 1-inch pieces

1 pint cherry tomatoes

3 tablespoons fresh lime juice

1 tablespoon olive oil

3/4 teaspoon sugar

salt and freshly ground pepper to taste

1/4 cup torn fresh mint leaves

● Prepare a grill for barbecue, brushing the rack with vegetable oil. Trim the ends from the cucumber. Cut cucumber in half lengthwise. Cut halves crosswise into 3/4-inch chunks. Thread cucumbers, scallions, and tomatoes onto skewers and grill over a medium-hot fire, turning occasionally, until scallions and tomatoes are evenly charred, about 5 minutes.

● Whisk the lime juice, olive oil, sugar, salt, and pepper in a shallow bowl until the sugar is dissolved. Slide the cucumber, scallions, and tomatoes off the skewers into the dressing. Add the mint and toss to mix.

PER SERVING: 61 CALORIES; 2 G PROTEIN; 9 G CARBOHYDRATES; 3 G TOTAL FAT; 0 G SATURATED FAT; 0 MG CHOLESTEROL; 14 MG SODIUM

COOKS' TIP:

You can use 3 Kirby cucumbers instead of the European seedless variety.

(SALAD) PREP TIME: 20 MINUTES   COOKING TIME: 25 MINUTES   (DRESSING) PREP TIME: 5 MINUTES

Leek and Potato Salad with Spicy Buttermilk Dressing

MAKES 6 SERVINGS

In a pinch, use canned potatoes—you don't have to parboil them. Rinse them before using.

extra virgin olive oil for grill and vegetables
1 pound small, new red potatoes
1 pound leeks, trimmed and washed
Spicy Buttermilk Dressing, recipe follows

• Prepare a grill for barbecuing. Oil a vegetable grilling pan and place on the grill to preheat. With a vegetable peeler, remove a strip of skin from around each potato. Cook potatoes and leeks in a large saucepan of boiling, salted water 10 minutes. Drain in a colander. Return to the saucepan and drizzle with a little oil; toss to coat.

• Oil the grill rack. Place the potatoes in the pre-heated grill pan and the leeks on the grill with the leeks perpendicular to the grill grids so they won't fall through. Grill over medium-high heat until tender, 10 to 15 minutes, turning every 2 minutes. Remove to a cutting board. Cut the potatoes in half and the leeks into 1-inch pieces. Place in a bowl and toss with enough dressing to coat.

Spicy Buttermilk Dressing

MAKES ABOUT 1 CUP

A homemade dressing boosts a salad to a status item everyone wants to try. You can also use this one as a dip for crudités or a drizzle over fresh tomatoes.

1/4 cup buttermilk
1/4 cup wasabi- or chipotle-flavored mayonnaise
2 tablespoons whole milk or plain yogurt or
  sour cream
1 1/2 teaspoons cider vinegar
1/4 cup grapeseed or vegetable oil
1 large garlic clove, crushed through a press
2 tablespoons snipped chives
salt and freshly ground pepper to taste

• In a medium bowl, whisk the buttermilk, mayonnaise, milk, and vinegar until smooth. In a thin, steady stream, whisk in the oil. Stir in the garlic and chives and season with salt and pepper.

SALAD WITHOUT DRESSING, PER SERVING: 127 CALORIES; 3 G PROTEIN;
24 G CARBOHYDRATES; 3 G TOTAL FAT; 0 G SATURATED FAT;
0 MG CHOLESTEROL; 20 MG SODIUM
DRESSING, PER SERVING: 129 CALORIES; 0 G PROTEIN; 3 G CARBOHYDRATES;
13 G TOTAL FAT; 1 G SATURATED FAT; 3 MG CHOLESTEROL;
179 MG SODIUM

COOKS' TIP:

You can use reconstituted powdered buttermilk; it's available in the baking section of most grocery stores.

PREP TIME: 20 MINUTES COOKING TIME: 10 MINUTES

Warm Salmon Salad with Yuzu Vinaigrette

MAKES 4 SERVINGS

Tamari sauce is available at Japanese grocery stores; it's a soy sauce made with soy beans and rice instead of soy beans and wheat.

4 center-cut salmon fillets, about 1^1/2-inches thick, with skin (8 ounces each) (It's okay to use skinned, thinner fish, but you will have to cook them several minutes less per side)

1^1/2 tablespoons white miso

^{1}/3 cup yuzu (citron juice, available at Japanese grocery stores) or 2^1/2 tablespoons fresh lemon juice and 3 tablespoons fresh orange juice

2^1/2 tablespoons grated peeled fresh gingerroot

^{1}/2 teaspoon Asian sesame oil

1^1/2 teaspoons tamari sauce

^{1}/4 cup extra virgin olive oil and more for the grill

2 tablespoons snipped chives

freshly ground pepper

^{1}/2 pound mesclun greens

COOKS' TIP:

The salad also goes well with grilled chicken or shrimp.

• Prepare a grill for barbecuing. Place the salmon on a foil-lined baking sheet and rub with ^{1}/2 tablespoon of miso. In a bowl, mix 1^1/2 tablespoons of yuzu juice, 1^1/2 tablespoons of gingerroot, and the sesame oil. Add the salmon and turn to coat; let stand for 10 minutes.

• Meanwhile, prepare vinaigrette: In a bowl, mix the remaining 1 tablespoon of miso with the remaining 1 tablespoon of gingerroot. Whisk in the remaining yuzu juice and the tamari, then whisk in the olive oil. Add the chives and season with pepper.

• Oil the grill and add the salmon, skin side down. Cover the grill and cook the salmon over medium-high heat for 4 to 6 minutes, depending on the thickness of the fillets. Gently turn over the salmon fillets and grill for 2 to 4 minutes longer, or until the salmon is just cooked through. Transfer the salmon to a plate and keep warm.

• Toss the mesclun greens with half the vinaigrette and arrange on a serving platter or individual plates. Top with the fillets. Drizzle with remaining vinaigrette and serve immediately.

PER SERVING: 491 CALORIES; 60 G PROTEIN; 5 G CARBOHYDRATES; 25 G TOTAL FAT; 3 G SATURATED FAT; 142 MG CHOLESTEROL; 562 MG SODIUM

PREP TIME: 10 MINUTES   COOKING TIME: 6 MINUTES

Grilled Fruit Salad

MAKES 4 SERVINGS

You can use the last of your coals to cook the fruit until tender and with a flavorful, sweet intensity. Use any leftovers to top slices of toasted pound cake or angel food cake.

1 peach, halved and pitted

1 nectarine, halved and pitted

1 red plum, halved and pitted

1 black plum, halved and pitted

2 rings (1-inch thick) of fresh pineapple, cored

1/2 cup sweetened condensed milk

1/4 cup bottled citrus vinaigrette

1 tablespoon grated peeled fresh gingerroot

1/2 teaspoon cinnamon, plus extra for dusting

grapeseed oil for the grill and the fruit

mascarpone or fresh goat cheese for serving

mint sprigs for garnish

● Prepare a grill for barbecuing. Place fruit on a foil-lined baking sheet. Mix the milk, vinaigrette, gingerroot, and cinnamon together in a glass measuring cup. Lightly oil the cut sides of the fruit halves and both flat sides of the pineapple rings.

● Oil the grill and add the fruit, in batches, as it cooks quickly. Cook fruit 1 minute; turn over and grill 45 seconds longer. Brush cut sides with milk mixture; turn over and grill until milk mixture has caramelized, about 30 seconds. Remove fruit to a cutting board; repeat with remaining fruit and milk mixture.

● Cut the fruit into bite-size pieces and arrange on plates or in shallow bowls. Serve with a dollop of mascarpone alongside; dust it with cinnamon. Garnish the fruit with mint.

PER SERVING: 186 CALORIES; 3 G PROTEIN; 29 G CARBOHYDRATES;
8 G TOTAL FAT; 2 G SATURATED FAT; 9 MG CHOLESTEROL; 110 MG SODIUM

COOKS' TIP:

Even skewers of a variety of grapes will make a tasty salad. Double-skewer them crosswise and grilled until charred.

PREP TIME: 10 MINUTES   COOKING TIME: 5 MINUTES

Shrimp Salad with Green Goddess Dressing

MAKES 6 SERVINGS

Time equals money, and you will spend enough time peeling and deveining even large shrimp to warrant buying them ready-to-go. But if you have time, grill the shrimp in their shells one day and peel them when you have time later or the next morning. Shrimp cooked in their shells will not dry out as much as "naked" ones, so their juiciness is worth the effort.

1 mango
1½ pounds large shrimp, peeled and deveined
1 bunch fat scallions, trimmed and cut into 1-inch
  pieces
Green Goddess Dressing, recipe follows

• Prepare a grill for barbecuing. Soak 10 wooden skewers in hot water. Cut mango in half lengthwise, going around the long pit in the center. Repeat with the other half so the pit is free. Cut off the skin around the pit section and, working over a bowl, cut the fruit into chunks. Place the chunks in the bowl. Score the flesh of the outside halves of the mango to the skin, but not through it, with a paring knife into 1-inch pieces. Pop out the squares by pressing on the skin and cut off the squares. Add them to the bowl and toss to coat with juices. Place shrimp, scallions, and mango in separate bowls and drizzle each with dressing. Toss to coat and thread each ingredient onto skewers. Grill over high heat, cooking the mango about 2 minutes, and the shrimp and scallions 5 minutes, until cooked through and charred.

• Unthread the shrimp, scallions, and mango into large bowl and toss to mix. Spoon onto serving dishes or shallow bowls and pass the dressing separately to drizzle as desired.

SALAD, WITHOUT DRESSING, PER SERVING: 196 CALORIES; 24 G PROTEIN;
10 G CARBOHYDRATES; 7 G TOTAL FAT; 1 G SATURATED FAT;
172 MG CHOLESTEROL; 250 MG SODIUM

Green Goddess Dressing

MAKES 6 SERVINGS, ABOUT 1¹/2 CUPS

This creation of the chef at San Francisco's Palace Hotel in the 1920s was made as a tribute to George Arliss, an actor in a local production of a play called "Green Goddess." Homemade mayonnaise makes it even more special, if you have the time to make some.

1/2 *ripe avocado, cut into 1-inch chunks*

3/4 *cup mayonnaise*

1 small shallot, minced

1 garlic clove, crushed through a press

3 tablespoons chopped flat-leaf parsley

1 tablespoon chopped tarragon

1 tablespoon chopped basil

1 tablespoon chopped cilantro

1 tablespoon snipped chives

salt and freshly ground pepper to taste

fresh lemon juice to taste

fresh lime juice to taste

hot water, if needed

● In a food processor, process the avocado until evenly chopped. Add the mayonnaise and process until just smooth; be careful to not overdo it. Scrape mixture into a bowl. Stir in the shallot, garlic, and herbs and whisk until blended. Season with salt, pepper, and lemon and lime juices. Thin with hot water to desired consistency.

PER SERVING: 147 CALORIES; 1 G PROTEIN; 9 G CARBOHYDRATES; 13 G TOTAL FAT; 2 G SATURATED FAT; 8 MG CHOLESTEROL; 213 MG SODIUM

COOKS' TIP:

The dressing makes a delicious dip for crudités or breadsticks and it also is used as a sauce for fish.

Grilled Waldorf Salad with Mint

MAKES 6 SERVINGS

Taking liberty with the classic 1890s composition from New York's Waldorf-Astoria Hotel, this version contains grilled celery and spiced apples tossed with a vinaigrette instead of mayonnaise.

oil for brushing the grill
2 Granny Smith apples
2 McIntosh apples
2 celery stalks
4 tablespoons butter, melted
1 tablespoon cinnamon sugar
1/3 cup firmly packed torn fresh mint leaves
1/4 cup golden raisins
1/4 cup toasted pecans
1/4 cup bottled citrus vinaigrette dressing
salt and freshly ground black pepper
6 Bibb or Boston lettuce leaves for serving

COOKS' TIP:

Garnish the salad with the tender yellow inner leaves of celery.

- Prepare a grill for barbecuing and brush the rack with oil. Oil a vegetable grilling pan and place on the grill. Wash the apples and quarter lengthwise. Core and cut each quarter in half lengthwise. Place the slices and the celery in a single layer on a foil-lined baking sheet. Brush the celery with some butter. Mix the remaining butter and cinnamon sugar in a cup and brush over the apples.

- Grill the celery directly on the grill and place the apples in the preheated pan. Cook over medium-low heat until tender when pierced with a thin skewer, about 10 minutes, turning after 5 minutes. Transfer the apple slices and celery to a cutting board and cut into bite-size pieces. Place in a bowl, add the mint, raisins, pecans, and dressing; toss to mix. Taste and season with salt and pepper.

- Spoon salad into 6 lettuce leaves, place on plates, and serve warm or at room temperature.

PER SERVING: 232 CALORIES; 1 G PROTEIN; 23 G CARBOHYDRATES; 16 G TOTAL FAT; 6 G SATURATED FAT; 21 MG CHOLESTEROL; 265 MG SODIUM

PREP TIME: 15 MINUTES   COOKING TIME: 15 MINUTES

Deconstructed Salad Niçoise

MAKES 6 SERVINGS

The classic French mix of fresh summer ingredients has never lost its appeal, but a visual makeover broadens its audience.

4 fresh tuna steaks, 1-inch thick (6 ounces each)
1/2 cup bottled lemon or other citrus vinaigrette
  dressing
1 pound small, new potatoes
6 ounces yellow wax beans, ends trimmed
6 ounces green beans, ends trimmed
1 Kirby cucumber, diced
1/2 cup red pear tomatoes
1/2 cup yellow pear tomatoes
1/4 cup pitted Niçoise olives, or small pitted
  black olives
6 cups mesclun greens
2 hard-cooked eggs, cut into wedges
coarse sea salt and freshly cracked pepper

• Prepare a grill for barbecuing. Heat 2 quarts salted water to boiling in a 3-quart saucepan. Place the tuna in a shallow dish and pour 1/4 cup of the dressing on top. Turn steaks to coat. Set aside. Place a vegetable grill pan on the grill to preheat.

• Add potatoes and beans to the boiling water and cook until half done, no more than 4 minutes. Drain in a colander, rinse with cold water, and place in a large bowl. Drizzle with 2 tablespoons dressing and toss to coat. Place in the preheated grill pan and cook over high heat, turning occasionally, until evenly browned and cooked through, about 5 minutes.

• Combine the cucumber, tomatoes, and olives in the bowl used for the potatoes and beans. Add remaining dressing; toss to coat.

• Drain the tuna, reserving marinade. Place in a hinged grill rack, and grill over high heat 4 to 6 minutes per side for medium rare. Remove to a cutting board; loosely cover with foil.

• Place the greens on four large dinner plates; top with the potatoes and beans. Slice the tuna on the diagonal and lift the steak, keeping the slices together, onto the salad. Fan out the slices slightly and top with cucumber mixture. Spoon any dressing remaining in bowl on top. Garnish with the egg and sprinkle with sea salt and cracked pepper.

PER SERVING: 345 CALORIES; 35 G PROTEIN; 23 G CARBOHYDRATES;
13 G TOTAL FAT; 2 G SATURATED FAT; 105 MG CHOLESTEROL; 723 MG SODIUM

COOKS' TIP:

You can use little quail eggs instead of chicken eggs. Simmer them for 5 minutes in boiling water and rinse until cool enough to peel.

PREP TIME: 15 MINUTES   COOKING TIME: 23 MINUTES

Warm Pasta Salad with Lemon Chicken and Mushrooms

MAKES 4 SERVINGS

As with most food trends, pasta salads enjoyed a heyday and then went away quietly. Warm pasta salads are still enjoyed because they are juicier and more fragrant than cold versions. This one can be turned into a hot main dish by serving it immediately, with some hot pasta water to moisten the Parmiagiano Reggiano cheese and turn it into a tasty sauce.

olive oil for the grill
1/2 pound penne, farfalle, or rotelle pasta
1/2 pound cremini mushrooms, halved lengthwise
3 tablespoons fresh lemon juice
salt and freshly ground pepper
1/4 cup bottled garlic Caesar salad dressing
1 pound skinless, boneless chicken breast halves
1 red bell pepper, thinly sliced
1/2 cup chopped basil
1/2 cup freshly grated Parmigiano Reggiano cheese

COOKS' TIP:

Use a mix of mushrooms such as Portobello, enoki, and shiitake.

● Prepare a grill for barbecuing. Oil a vegetable grill pan and set on the grill to preheat. In a large saucepan of boiling salted water, cook the pasta, stirring occasionally, until al dente. Drain and transfer to a large bowl. Keep warm.

● Meanwhile, brush the cut sides of the mushrooms with 1 tablespoon of the lemon juice and season with salt and pepper. Place the mushrooms in the prepared grill pan and cook over a medium-high heat until lightly charred and tender, 3 to 5 minutes. Add the mushrooms to the pasta.

● Mix the remaining lemon juice with the dressing. Brush the chicken breasts with 2 teaspoons of the dressing and season with salt and pepper. Grill the chicken until cooked through over medium-high heat, turning once, about 10 minutes. Transfer the chicken to a platter and let stand for 5 minutes.

● Cut the chicken into bite-size pieces and add them to the pasta mixture. Add the red pepper and the remaining dressing and toss well. Sprinkle the basil and cheese on top, adjust seasonings, toss again, and serve.

PER SERVING: 487 CALORIES; 41 G PROTEIN; 50 G CARBOHYDRATES; 13 G TOTAL FAT; 4 G SATURATED FAT; 76 MG CHOLESTEROL; 574 MG SODIUM

(SALAD) PREP TIME: 15 MINUTES   COOKING TIME: 20 MINUTES   (DRESSING) PREP TIME: 5 MINUTES

Ham and Pineapple Salad with Sweet and Spicy Ginger Dressing

MAKES 4 SERVINGS

This salad joins together many of ham's best buddies: grilled pineapple, crunchy cabbage slaw, ginger, and cheese. The mixture can be made ahead of time and refrigerated. Let it stand at room temperature for about 15 minutes before serving.

1 ham steak (1/2 pound)
1 ripe pineapple, peeled, cored, and sliced into
    3/4-inch thick rings
Sweet and Spicy Ginger Dressing, recipe follows
1 bag shredded coleslaw mix (10 ounces), with
    red and green cabbage and carrots
1 cup shredded extra-sharp Cheddar cheese

• Prepare a grill for barbecuing. Place ham and pineapple on a foil-lined baking sheet and brush on both sides with some of the dressing. Place ham and pineapple on the grill over medium-low heat and grill until hot and caramelized, 15 to 20 minutes, turning once after 8 minutes. Remove to a cutting board and cut into large, bite-size pieces. Place in a large bowl and drizzle with some dressing. Toss to coat.

• Place the coleslaw mixture into a salad bowl and drizzle with the dressing. Toss to coat. Spoon onto large plates or shallow bowls. Top with the ham and pineapple and sprinkle with some cheese.

Sweet and Spicy Ginger Dressing

MAKES ABOUT 1/2 CUP

This dressing is a versatile blend of flavors and also makes a delicious marinade for fish, shrimp, and chicken.

3 tablespoons minced peeled fresh gingerroot
3 tablespoons low-sodium soy sauce
1 tablespoon sugar
1 tablespoon peanut oil
1 tablespoon mirin (sweet rice wine)
1/2 teaspoon distilled white vinegar
1/2 teaspoon Asian sesame oil
1/2 teaspoon crushed red pepper

• Place ingredients in a jar with a tight-fitting lid and shake until the sugar is dissolved.

SALAD, WITHOUT DRESSING, PER SERVING: 294 CALORIES; 18 G PROTEIN;
21 G CARBOHYDRATES; 16 G TOTAL FAT; 8 G SATURATED FAT;
62 MG CHOLESTEROL; 937 MG SODIUM
DRESSING, PER SERVING: 59 CALORIES; 0 G PROTEIN; 4 G CARBOHYDRATES;
5 G TOTAL FAT; 0 G SATURATED FAT; 0 MG CHOLESTEROL; 257 MG SODIUM

COOKS' TIPS:

• You can use canned pineapple rings, packed in syrup or natural juices, instead of the fresh fruit.

• Make a double batch and store the remainder in the refrigerator.

Fish & Shellfish

Squid Kebabs with Zucchini and Lemon •

Sofrito-Grilled Mackerel •

Halibut Packets with •
Onions, Oranges, and Olives

Sea Scallops on the Half Shell •

Garlic-Grilled Calamari and Fennel •

Salmon Kebabs with •
Sherry Vinegar Dipping Sauce

Catfish and Okra with Coconut-Curry •
Tomato Sauce

Meal-in-a-Packet Sea Bass with Bok Choy •

• Seared Scallop Kebabs over Squid Pasta

• Soft-Shell Crabs
with Chinese Black Bean Sauce

• Bluefish Tacos

• Tartared Bluefish

• Tuna with Caper-Butter Sauce

• Mustard-Coated Salmon with
Tomato-Paprika Butter

• Prosciutto-Wrapped Crab Cakes

• Creole-Style Catfish

• Soy-Glazed Shrimp and Water Chestnuts

Squid Kebabs with Zucchini and Lemon

MAKES 6 SERVINGS

Skewered grilled squid is especially popular in Japan and China, where it is enjoyed as everyday "street food."

1 pound small (4 inches) cleaned squid

4 small (1-inch diameter) zucchini, cut crosswise into 1/2-inch rounds

2 lemons, cut into 1/2-inch thick rounds, each quartered, plus extra lemon wedges for squeezing

3 tablespoons olive oil

1 large garlic clove, crushed through a press

salt and freshly ground pepper

1/2 cup butter, partially melted

chopped parsley and oregano for serving

COOKS' TIP:

You can use shrimp or scallops (sea or bay) instead of the squid. Keep them whole and arrange lengthwise on the skewers.

• Prepare a grill for barbecuing. Soak 12 eight-inch wooden skewers in water for 20 minutes.

• Cut the squid heads crosswise into 1-inch thick rings, and the tentacles into pieces. Thread 4 or 5 pieces onto each skewer, alternating with zucchini (skewered through the skin) and lemon wedges (skewered through the skin), ending with a tentacle portion. Place on a foil-lined baking sheet. Mix olive oil with the garlic and season generously with salt and pepper. Brush the garlic mixture over the kebabs. Set aside.

• Grill kebabs over a hot fire until lightly charred and just cooked, about 1 minute each side. Place kebabs on warm plates and place a dollop of the butter alongside for dipping. Sprinkle the kebabs and butter with the chopped herbs.

PER SERVING: 109 CALORIES; 13 G PROTEIN; 9 G CARBOHYDRATES; 4 G TOTAL FAT; 0.5 G SATURATED FAT; 176 MG CHOLESTEROL; 133 MG SODIUM

PREP TIME: 20 MINUTES   COOKING TIME: 4 MINUTES

Sofrito-Grilled Mackerel

MAKES 4 SERVINGS

Packed with nutritious omega-3 oil, mackerel is one of the best fish to grill because the natural fat in the flesh allows it to cook without drying out as easily as other fish.

1/3 cup fresh lime juice

2 tablespoons olive oil, plus extra for the grill

2 tablespoons sofrito, recipe follows

4 mackerel fillets, 3/4-inch thick
   (about 1 1/2 pounds total)

1/4 cup finely chopped scallions

1 tablespoon honey

1 tablespoon water

• Prepare a grill for barbecuing. Mix the lime juice, oil, and sofrito in a bowl and remove 1/4 cup to a smaller bowl. Place a hinged fish-grilling rack on a foil-lined baking sheet and brush with oil. Place the fish in the rack and brush on both sides with 1/4 cup of the sofrito mixture. Let stand 10 minutes. Meanwhile, mix the scallions, honey, and water into the remaining sofrito mixture and set aside.

• Grill the fish 6 inches from hot coals, 2 minutes on each side or until cooked through. Serve with the reserved sofrito mixture.

Homemade Sofrito
MAKES 8 SERVINGS

You can buy bottled sofrito in the Hispanic foods section of the grocery store, but it's easy to make. Each cook has a "house blend" but this recipe is basic.

1/4 cup vegetable oil

1 cup chopped onion

1 cup chopped green bell pepper

4 cloves garlic, crushed

3/4 cup chopped tomatoes

1 tablespoon red wine vinegar

salt and freshly ground pepper to taste

• Heat oil in a skillet over medium heat and fry onion, pepper, and garlic until onion is lightly browned, about 4 minutes. Add the tomatoes and cook rapidly while stirring over medium-high heat until liquid has evaporated and mixture is thick, about 1 minute. Stir in the vinegar. Cook 1 minute and season with salt and pepper.

FISH, PER SERVING: 450 CALORIES; 33 G PROTEIN; 7 G CARBOHYDRATES; 32 G TOTAL FAT; 6 G SATURATED FAT; 119 MG CHOLESTEROL; 294 MG SODIUM SOFRITO, PER SERVING: 78 CALORIES; 1 G PROTEIN; 4 G CARBOHYDRATES; 7 G TOTAL FAT; 1 G SATURATED FAT; 0 MG CHOLESTEROL; 147 MG SODIUM

PREP TIME: 15 MINUTES   COOKING TIME: 18 MINUTES

Halibut Packets with Onions, Oranges, and Olives

MAKES 4 SERVINGS

Berbere is an Ethopian spice mix that combines garlic with several dry spices that include hot pepper and cardamom. It is available at Middle Eastern grocery stores.

extra virgin olive oil

4 thick, skinless halibut fillets (8 ounces each)

1 red onion, peeled and cut crosswise into
  1/2-inch slices; keep slices intact

1 navel orange

salt

1/2 cup oil-cured black olives (about 3 ounces),
  pitted and coarsely chopped

1/4 cup finely shredded mint

pinch of berbere, or smoked hot Spanish paprika, or
  cayenne pepper, or Maryland-style seafood
  seasoning

• Prepare a grill for barbecuing. Soak eight thin wooden skewers in hot water. Arrange four 18-inch-long pieces of foil on a work surface and lightly brush the center of each with a little olive oil. Place a halibut fillet on top of each.

• Oil the grill. Place onion slices, intact, on a foil-lined baking sheet. Insert skewers through the side of the layers of onion slices to keep the rings intact. Remove the orange zest in strips with a vegetable peeler and shred into very fine strips, enough to measure 2 tablespoons. Remove the remaining zest, along with the white pith. Cut the orange crosswise into 8 thin rounds, and carefully remove the seeds. Place the rounds on the same foil-lined baking sheet with the onions.

• Brush both sides of the onions and oranges with oil and sprinkle lightly with salt. Grill onion and orange slices on both sides over medium-high heat until tender and charred, about 8 minutes in all for the onions and 2 minutes for the oranges. Remove the oranges and onions to a cutting board as they are done. Remove skewers from the onions. Slide an orange slice on each halibut fillet, top with an onion layer, and top with another orange slice. Separate the rings from the remaining onion layers and divide in each packet. Sprinkle with the olives, mint, orange zest strips, and berbere. Fold up the foil over the fish and seasonings and seal to make a packet.

• Place packets on the grill and cook over medium heat 10 minutes, when you can first hear the juices boiling. Remove the packets to large plates. Carefully open the packets to avoid the hot steam. Or, carefully make a small slit in the side of each packet and pour the juices into each of 4 large, shallow soup bowls. Using a spatula, lift the fish and vegetables into the juices.

PER SERVING: 281 CALORIES; 48 G PROTEIN; 4 G CARBOHYDRATES; 7 G TOTAL FAT; 1 G SATURATED FAT; 73 MG CHOLESTEROL; 368 MG SODIUM

COOKS' TIP:

The concentrated flavor of dried, oil-cured olives is surprising if one is used to eating the soft, mild black olives from California or even a Greek Kalamata or French Niçoise olive. The bitterness is only momentary, though, as the olive flavor unfolds and mixes in with the sweetness of the orange and spiciness of the mint.

PREP TIME: 10 MINUTES   COOKING TIME: 12 MINUTES

Sea Scallops on the Half Shell

MAKES 4 SERVINGS

If you can't get fresh sea scallops in their shells, you can pile loose sea or bay scallops or a mixture of scallops and cubed fish fillets such as salmon, catfish, and halibut, on purchased large scallop shells available at kitchen supply shops. The simplicity of the perfectly cooked seafood, dressed with a bit of tangy accents, makes this an easy and elegant dish.

*12 sea scallops, removed from their shells, tough
    muscle cut off, shells reserved*
lime wedges
2 tablespoons Chinese sweet chili sauce (optional)

• Prepare a grill for barbecuing. Rinse scallops thoroughly to remove grains of sand. Place scallops, each on a shell, on a baking sheet and squeeze a little lime juice over each. Grill scallops, on their shells, over medium-high heat just until firm, 10 to 12 minutes. Serve with a little chili sauce, if you like.

PER SERVING: 225 CALORIES; 43 G PROTEIN; 6 G CARBOHYDRATES; 2 G TOTAL FAT; 0.2 G SATURATED FAT; 84 MG CHOLESTEROL; 410 MG SODIUM

Garlic-Grilled Calamari and Fennel

MAKES 6 SERVINGS

Be sure not to overcook the squid; if they are small, skewer them separately from the fennel and cook them only 1 minute on each side or they will get tough.

2 small fennel bulbs, trimmed and cut into wedges

3 garlic cloves, crushed through a press

1/3 cup extra virgin olive oil

2 tablespoons finely chopped flat-leaf parsley

1/4 cup fresh lemon juice, plus lemon wedges
 for serving

pinch of crushed red pepper flakes

salt and freshly ground pepper

1 1/2 pounds cleaned small (3-inch) calamari (squid)

COOKS' TIP:

For the best flavor, it is best to buy fresh squid the day you are going to cook it.

- Prepare a grill for barbecuing. Finely snip the ferns from the fennel into a bowl. Add the garlic, oil, parsley, lemon juice, and red pepper flakes and season well with salt and pepper. Mix well.

- Trim the stalks and ends from the fennel bulbs, keeping the bulbs intact. Cut each bulb lengthwise into 8 wedges, keeping the layers intact.

- Double-skewer the calamari and fennel pieces and place on a rimmed baking sheet. Brush well with the garlic mixture on all sides. (As an alternative to skewering the squid and fennel, brush them with the garlic mixture and place in a shallow hinged basket.)

- Grill the squid and fennel over medium-high heat until tender and lightly charred, about 4 minutes, turning and basting with the remaining garlic mixture every minute. Serve with lemon wedges.

PER SERVING: 244 CALORIES; 19 G PROTEIN; 11 G CARBOHYDRATES;
14 G TOTAL FAT; 1 G SATURATED FAT; 264 MG CHOLESTEROL; 188 MG SODIUM

Salmon Kebabs with Sherry Vinegar Dipping Sauce

MAKES 4 SERVINGS

The fat from the applewood-smoked bacon is the only seasoning the fish needs while cooking. The dipping sauce supplies the finishing touch.

8 strips applewood-smoked bacon

2 1/2 pounds skinless salmon fillets, cut into 1-inch
    cubes (about 16 cubes)

2 tablespoons torn fresh mint leaves

2 tablespoons extra virgin olive oil, plus extra for grill

2 tablespoons sherry vinegar

2 tablespoons fresh orange juice

• Prepare a grill for barbecuing. Soak eight thin wooden skewers in hot water. Cut bacon strips in half crosswise; wrap one half around each piece of salmon. Thread salmon onto skewers twice to keep them from spinning around on the skewers.

• Oil the grill rack. Place skewers on grill rack and grill, covered, until bacon is crisp and salmon is barely cooked through, about 4 minutes, turning after 2 minutes.

• While salmon cooks, whisk mint with oil, vinegar, and orange juice in small bowl. Use as a dipping sauce for salmon chunks.

PER SERVING: 328 CALORIES; 28 G PROTEIN; 1 G CARBOHYDRATES; 23 G TOTAL FAT; 4 G SATURATED FAT; 81 MG CHOLESTEROL; 251 MG SODIUM

COOKS' TIP:

Make up a triple batch of the dipping sauce, pour out one-third to use for the kebabs, and store the remainder in the refrigerator. It makes a nice deglazing mixture for pan-fried calves' liver or sautéed mushrooms.

PREP TIME: 10 MINUTES   COOKING TIME: 18 MINUTES

Catfish and Okra with Coconut-Curry Tomato Sauce

MAKES 4 SERVINGS

Grilled catfish is tied with fried catfish for flavor, as many anglers of the bottom feeders would agree. But grilled okra alongside fried? That may be the next revelation!

3 tablespoons peanut or canola oil, plus extra
  for brushing
1 tablespoon mild curry powder
1 tablespoon fresh gingerroot, peeled and grated
4 catfish fillets (3/4-inch thick)
6 ounces small okra, stem ends barely trimmed
1 can (16 ounces) diced tomatoes with jalapeño
1 cup unsweetened coconut milk
1/2 teaspoon sugar
salt and freshly ground pepper
2 tablespoons chopped cilantro

COOKS' TIP:

Be sure to use Thai or Thai-style coconut milk, not the coconut cream you use for piña coladas.

● Prepare a grill for barbecuing. Combine 2 tablespoons oil, 1 1/2 teaspoons of the curry powder, and 1 1/2 teaspoons gingerroot in a cup and mix well. Place catfish fillets and okra on a foil-lined baking sheet. Brush catfish on both sides with oil mixture. Brush okra, a vegetable grill pan, and a hinged grill rack with oil. Place fish in the oiled grill rack. Preheat the grill pan on the grill.

● Heat 1 tablespoon oil in a small saucepan over medium-high heat until simmering. Remove from the heat and add the remaining curry powder and gingerroot. Stir until fragrant. Return pan to the heat and add the tomatoes, coconut milk, and sugar. Heat to boiling, stirring; season with salt and pepper and simmer until thickened, about 10 minutes.

● Grill catfish over medium-high heat about 8 minutes, until cooked through, turning rack after 4 minutes. Grill okra in vegetable grill pan alongside the fish, turning with tongs, until charred and tender.

● Stir the cilantro into the tomato sauce and serve with the fish and okra.

PER SERVING: 500 CALORIES; 31 G PROTEIN; 15 G CARBOHYDRATES;
37 G TOTAL FAT; 15 G SATURATED FAT; 80 MG CHOLESTEROL; 253 MG SODIUM

Meal-in-a-Packet Sea Bass with Bok Choy

MAKES 4 SERVINGS

Steamed in foil over hot coals, fish is guaranteed to be moist and fragrant. The colorful mix of vegetables makes each packet extra nutritious, for all the water-soluble vitamins go into the juices.

1 tablespoon butter, softened

2 ounces sliced pancetta, diced

1/2 pound sliced mushrooms

1 bunch scallions, trimmed, thinly sliced

1 head baby bok choy (6 ounces), coarsely shredded

1 small red bell pepper, seeded and sliced in
   thin strips

1 small yellow bell pepper, seeded and sliced
   in thin strips

1/2 package shredded carrots (4 ounces total)

freshly ground pepper

1/4 cup fresh lemon juice

2 tablespoons low-sodium soy sauce

4 skinless sea bass fillets (8 ounces each)

COOKS' TIP:

You can make up the packets in the morning and chill them until about 15 minutes before cooking. Depending on the density of the pack, the chilling may add 2 to 3 minutes to cooking time.

• Prepare a grill for barbecuing. Tear off four 18-inch lengths of foil. Generously brush the softened butter over an 8-inch square in the center of each foil sheet. Set aside.

• Sauté the pancetta in a large skillet over medium-high heat until browned, about 3 minutes. Add the mushrooms and scallions and sauté until tender, about 5 minutes. Add the bok choy, red and yellow peppers, and carrots. Cover, and steam 4 minutes. Season the mixture with pepper. Stir in the lemon juice and soy sauce.

• Place a piece of fish in the center of each sheet and top with the pancetta mixture and any juices. Fold the sides of the foil up around the fish to make sealed packets. Place on the grill and cook over medium heat 10 minutes, when you can first hear the juices boiling. Remove the packets to large plates. Carefully open the packets to avoid the hot steam. Or, carefully make a small slit in the side of each packet and pour the juices into each of 4 large, shallow soup bowls. Using a spatula, lift the fish and vegetables into the juices.

PER SERVING: 338 CALORIES; 48 G PROTEIN; 14 G CARBOHYDRATES; 15 G TOTAL FAT; 7 G SATURATED FAT; 119 MG CHOLESTEROL; 661 MG SODIUM

PREP TIME: 15 MINUTES   COOKING TIME: 12 MINUTES

Seared Scallop Kebabs over Squid Pasta

MAKES 6 SERVINGS

Make sure your scallops are fat—about 1¼ inches thick—or they may dry out. If you can't find thick ones, cut the cooking time to 1 minute per side.

¼ cup fresh lemon juice

1 garlic clove, crushed through a press

2 teaspoons kosher salt

2 teaspoons chopped fresh oregano or
   1 teaspoon dried oregano

½ cup extra virgin olive oil plus extra for the grill

freshly ground pepper

20 sea scallops, thoroughly rinsed to remove sand

1 small red pepper, seeded and cut into
   1-inch squares

1 small yellow pepper, seeded and cut into
   1-inch squares

1 pound dried squid pasta

fresh basil leaves for garnish

COOKS' TIP:

You don't have to use the dramatic black pasta that is colored with squid ink; it's just more of a contrast than yellowish egg pasta. Try spinach linguine, if you can find it, to add to the beauty of the finished dish.

• Prepare a grill for barbecuing. Soak eight thin wooden skewers in hot water. In a medium bowl, whisk the lemon juice, garlic, and salt until the salt dissolves. Stir in the oregano. Slowly whisk in the olive oil until blended and thickened. Season generously with pepper.

• Heat a large saucepan of salted water to boiling. Meanwhile, working over a foil-lined baking sheet, double-skewer the scallops through the sides, 5 to a parallel pair of skewers, alternating the scallops with squares of red and yellow peppers. Remove half the lemon-juice mixture to a small bowl and brush over all sides of the kebabs.

• Cook the pasta until al dente according to package directions. Drain and keep warm. Cook the kebabs over high heat (as close to the heat as possible) 4 minutes in all, turning after 2 minutes and brushing with any remaining brushing sauce, or until charred and opaque. Be careful not to overcook, or scallops will become tough.

• Place the pasta in a large bowl and add the reserved lemon-juice mixture. Toss to coat. Unthread the skewers into the pasta and toss to mix. Garnish with basil leaves.

PER SERVING: 505 CALORIES; 19 G PROTEIN; 62 G CARBOHYDRATES; 20 G TOTAL FAT; 2 G SATURATED FAT; 17 MG CHOLESTEROL; 183 MG SODIUM

PREP TIME: 10 MINUTES   COOKING TIME: 8 MINUTES

Soft-Shell Crabs with Chinese Black Bean Sauce

MAKES 4 SERVINGS

The stage between the shedding of the crab's old hard shell and the forming of a new hard shell is called its soft-shell stage. The season used to be between April and mid-September, with a peak in June and July, but nowadays it seems that the crabs are never really out of season. The Chinese way of seasoning them is especially tasty.

8 medium soft-shell crabs, cleaned
2 tablespoons peanut oil, plus extra for the grill
2 tablespoons bottled Chinese black bean sauce
1/4 cup rice wine vinegar
1/2 teaspoon Chinese chili oil or a dash of Tabasco
chopped cilantro or whole leaves for garnish
lemon wedges, for serving

- Prepare a grill for barbecuing. Place the crabs on a foil-lined baking sheet. In a small bowl, mix 2 tablespoons oil, the bean sauce, vinegar, and chili oil. Brush some mixture over both sides of the crabs.

- Oil the grill. Grill the crabs top shell down over medium-high heat 4 minutes. Turn crabs over and cook 3 to 4 minutes, until shells turn red and legs are crisped.

- Place crabs on a platter. Sprinkle with cilantro and serve with lemon for squeezing.

PER SERVING: 121 CALORIES; 9 G PROTEIN; 2 G CARBOHYDRATES; 9 G TOTAL FAT; 1 G SATURATED FAT; 33 MG CHOLESTEROL; 758 MG SODIUM

Bluefish Tacos

MAKES 8 TACOS

This list of ingredients may seem long, but it doesn't reflect the ease of this recipe. As with any taco recipe, the sauce and add-ons make the meal a fiesta!

juice of 1 lime

1/4 cup corn oil, plus extra for the grill

1 cup torn cilantro leaves

1 teaspoon chili powder

1 pound bluefish fillets, skin removed

8 corn or flour tortillas

2 jarred or homemade roasted red peppers

1 chipotle chile in adobo sauce, or more to taste

1/3 cup sour cream or plain yogurt

salt and freshly ground pepper

1 cup bottled or fresh tomatillo salsa

shredded lettuce

*1 cup canned or homemade dried beans of
    choice, warmed*

bottled hot-pepper sauce to taste

COOKS' TIP:

Catfish makes a tasty grilled alternative to the bluefish.

● Prepare a grill for barbecuing. Combine the lime juice, 1/4 cup corn oil, 1/4 cup cilantro, and the chili powder in a shallow glass baking dish and mix well. Add the bluefish and turn to coat. Let stand while preparing the taco ingredients.

● Sprinkle a sheet of heavy-duty foil lightly with water and stack the tortillas on top. Sprinkle top with water. Wrap foil tightly around the tortillas and place to the side of the heated grill so that the tortillas will get warm, but not burn.

● Place the red peppers, chipotle chile and a little adobo sauce, and the sour cream in a food processor and process until smooth. Season with salt and pepper and place in a bowl. Set aside.

● Oil the grill. Turn the tortilla packet over. Drain the bluefish, reserving the marinade, and grill over medium-high heat 3 to 4 minutes. Brush with some of the reserved marinade and carefully turn over. Grill 1 to 3 minutes, until cooked through. Remove to a warm serving platter. Pull the fish apart along its natural divisions into bite-size chunks. Spoon into the warm tortillas and top with the roasted red-pepper sauce, tomatilla salsa, lettuce, beans, and hot sauce.

PER TACO: 255 CALORIES; 16 G PROTEIN; 22 G CARBOHYDRATES; 12 G TOTAL FAT; 2 G SATURATED FAT; 37 MG CHOLESTEROL; 390 MG SODIUM

PREP TIME: 10 MINUTES   COOKING TIME: 10 MINUTES

Tartared Bluefish

MAKES 4 SERVINGS

Coastal natives swear mayonnaise kills the fishy flavor that makes large "blues" a double-edged gift. Tartar sauce serves a double-duty when applied to the meaty flesh, adding a pickly piquancy. You might want to serve extra sauce on the side, as the specks of onion in it are nice with the fish.

2 pounds bluefish fillets, skin on, in 4 equal pieces
oil for brushing
salt and freshly ground black pepper
1/2 cup bottled or homemade tartar sauce
lemon wedges for serving

- Prepare a grill for barbecuing. Place the bluefish on a foil-lined baking sheet. Brush the skin side with oil and sprinkle with salt and pepper. Turn fillets over and slather the flesh side with the tartar sauce.

- Oil the grill rack. Grill the fish skin side down over high heat 4 to 6 minutes, until skin is crisped and the flesh is firm. Carefully turn fillets and grill 1 to 3 minutes, until cooked through. Serve skin side up, with lemon for squeezing.

PER SERVING: 432 CALORIES; 46 G PROTEIN; 8 G CARBOHYDRATES; 23 G TOTAL FAT; 4 G SATURATED FAT; 142 MG CHOLESTEROL; 375 MG SODIUM

COOKS' TIP:

Taylor blues, the smaller fish, are milder than the big, October catch. They are the way to go if you want to introduce your family and friends to the species.

Tuna with Caper-Butter Sauce

MAKES 6 SERVINGS

The buttery texture and flavor of tuna is brought out in this delicious recipe.

6 fresh yellowfin tuna steaks, at least 1-inch thick
   (about 1 1/2 pounds total)
1 stick (4 ounces) unsalted butter
1 jar (6 ounces) small capers, drained and rinsed
1 tablespoon coarse Dijon mustard
1 teaspoon grated lemon peel
2 tablespoons lemon juice or to taste
salt and freshly ground pepper

COOKS' TIP:

Instead of using tuna, you can substitute salmon, catfish, halibut, or bluefish, or even boneless chicken breasts. The caper-butter sauce is delicious with them all.

• Prepare a grill for barbecuing. Place tuna on a foil-lined baking sheet. Slowly melt butter in a small saucepan over medium-low heat and carefully pour off the clear top portion into a bowl, leaving behind the white milky portion. Add the capers, mustard, lemon peel, and 2 tablespoons lemon juice to the clarified butter in the bowl. Whisk until blended and taste. Season with salt, pepper, and more lemon juice, if needed. Spoon about 2 tablespoons of the mixture into a cup and brush some of the mixture over both sides of the tuna. Place remaining mixture in a saucepan and heat over medium-low heat.

• Grill tuna over medium-high heat 6 minutes, until flesh is lightly charred. Baste with remaining butter mixture in the cup and turn. Grill 4 to 6 minutes, to desired doneness. Serve with the remaining hot caper-butter sauce.

PER SERVING: 274 CALORIES; 30 G PROTEIN; 2 G CARBOHYDRATES;
17 G TOTAL FAT; 10 G SATURATED FAT; 75 MG CHOLESTEROL; 452 MG SODIUM

Mustard-Coated Salmon with Tomato-Paprika Butter

MAKES 4 SERVINGS

If you can't find salmon with the skin on, it's okay. Just be sure to spread the mustard mixture over all sides of the fish pieces. You don't coat the skin because it will not get crisp if you do.

4 salmon fillets with skin (6 ounces each)

2 tablespoons Dijon mustard

3 tablespoons extra virgin olive oil, plus extra for the grill

2 teaspoons fresh lemon juice

1 teaspoon soy sauce

1/2 teaspoon freshly ground pepper

Tomato-Paprika Butter, recipe follows

● Prepare a grill for barbecuing. Place the salmon on a plate. Mix mustard, 3 tablespoons oil, the lemon juice, soy sauce, and pepper and brush over the salmon, flesh only. Let stand 15 minutes.

● Oil the grill rack. Grill the salmon over medium-high heat, skin side down, 4 minutes, until the skin is crisp. Turn and grill until barely cooked through, about 8 minutes in all. Serve topped with a dollop of the Tomato-Paprika Butter.

Tomato-Paprika Butter

MAKES 8 SERVINGS

Plop a dollop of this flavorful mixture on hot steaks and corn on the cob or into bowls of steaming vegetables, noodles, or soup and watch it melt into a delicious "sauce."

1 stick (4 ounces) unsalted butter, softened

2 tablespoons sun-dried or regular tomato paste (homemade, canned, or from a tube)

1 tablespoon sweet paprika

1 teaspoon hot paprika

1 garlic clove, crushed through a press

kosher salt to taste

● In a medium bowl, whisk the butter with the tomato paste, paprikas, garlic, and salt.

FISH, PER SERVING: 384 CALORIES; 37 G PROTEIN; 2 G CARBOHYDRATES; 25 G TOTAL FAT; 4 G SATURATED FAT; 106 MG CHOLESTEROL; 253 MG SODIUM
TOMATO-PAPRIKA BUTTER, PER SERVING: 109 CALORIES; 1 G PROTEIN; 2 G CARBOHYDRATES; 12 G TOTAL FAT; 7 G SATURATED FAT; 31 MG CHOLESTEROL; 71 MG SODIUM

COOKS' TIP:

Store paprika and other peppers in the freezer or you may see some unwanted creatures as you go to shake or measure.

PREP TIME: 30 MINUTES   COOKING TIME: 8 MINUTES

Prosciutto-Wrapped Crab Cakes

MAKES 4 SERVINGS

Crab has a delicate texture and flavor and therefore is vulnerable to overcooking and over-seasoning. The ingredients here respect the quirks of the precious meat and the flavorful armor of prosciutto di Parma ham guarantees each cake a gentle steam-grilling.

2 large eggs, lightly beaten

1/4 cup wasabi-flavored or plain mayonnaise

1/4 cup minced scallions

1/2 teaspoon Worcestershire sauce

1/2 teaspoon dry mustard

1/4 teaspoon Tabasco

1 pound lump crabmeat, picked over

1/4 cup finely crushed buttery crackers

8 paper-thin slices prosciutto di Parma, halved
   lengthwise

4 tablespoons unsalted butter, melted

lemon wedges, for serving

COOKS' TIP:

If you can't find prosciutto di Parma, use packaged paper-thin dried beef.

• Prepare a grill for barbecuing. In a medium bowl, combine the eggs, mayonnaise, scallions, Worcestershire sauce, dry mustard, and Tabasco. Fold in the crabmeat and the cracker crumbs. Shape the mixture into 8 cakes about 1-inch thick. Wrap a half-slice of the prosciutto around the diameter of a crab cake as if, on a clock, from twelve to six o'clock; wrap another half-slice around the crab cake from three to nine o'clock. Repeat with remaining crab cakes and prosciutto. Place cakes on a foil-lined baking sheet, wrap with plastic wrap, and refrigerate at least 15 minutes. (Cakes may be made up hours in advance of cooking.)

• Oil the grill rack. Brush the top of the crab cakes with butter. Place buttered side down on the grill and cook over medium-high heat 3 to 4 minutes, until the prosciutto is crisped. Brush the remaining butter over the cakes and gently turn over. Cook 3 to 4 minutes, until the prosciutto is crisped and the cakes are hot. Remove to a platter and serve with lemon for squeezing.

PER SERVING: 387 CALORIES; 32 G PROTEIN; 6 G CARBOHYDRATES; 25 G TOTAL FAT; 10 G SATURATED FAT; 271 MG CHOLESTEROL; 930 MG SODIUM

PREP TIME: 10 MINUTES   COOKING TIME: 4 MINUTES

Creole-Style Catfish

MAKES 4 SERVINGS

Grilling fish is one of the best and simplest ways to show off its flavor and texture. A spicy coating "blackens" and gently stings the lips, making cold beer or lemonade a perfect accompaniment.

4 skinless catfish fillets (6 ounces each) or other firm
   fish fillets
3 tablespoons extra virgin olive oil, plus extra for
   the grill
1 tablespoon freshly ground black pepper
1 teaspoon kosher salt
1 1/2 teaspoons garlic powder
1 1/2 teaspoons paprika
1 teaspoon celery salt
1 teaspoon cayenne pepper
lime wedges, for serving

• Prepare a grill for barbecuing. Place catfish fillets on a foil-lined baking sheet and brush on both sides with oil. Mix the black pepper, salt, garlic powder, paprika, celery salt, and cayenne in a cup and pat onto both sides of fillets.

• Brush a hinged grill rack with oil and place fillets in the rack. Close and secure the handle and cook the fish over medium-high heat for 2 minutes per side, until crisp and cooked through. Transfer the fish to plates, garnish with lime wedges and serve.

PER SERVING: 260 CALORIES; 28 G PROTEIN; 1 G CARBOHYDRATES; 15 G TOTAL FAT; 2 G SATURATED FAT; 99 MG CHOLESTEROL; 940 MG SODIUM

PREP TIME: 15 MINUTES   COOKING TIME: 20 MINUTES

Soy-Glazed Shrimp and Water Chestnuts

MAKES 4 SERVINGS

Fresh gingerroot brightens everything it touches. Young ginger, with a greenish, paper-thin skin and tender—not fibrous—flesh is best, but if all that is available has dark brown skin, make sure it is not wrinkled or moldy. The mold penetrates the whole bulb, so it's best thrown out. To store the ginger, keep it dry in the crisper or peel it with a vegetable peeler, grate it, and store it in a jar, covered with dry sherry or vodka, in the refrigerator.

3 tablespoons peanut oil, plus extra for the grill

1/4 cup finely chopped peeled fresh gingerroot

1/4 cup low-sodium soy sauce

1/4 cup rice vinegar

2 tablespoons sugar

2 tablespoons sake or dry sherry

11/2 pounds large shrimp, shelled and deveined with tails intact

2 limes, cut into thin wedges

16 canned whole water chestnuts, rinsed and drained, or peeled, fresh water chestnuts

1 bunch thin scallions, trimmed and cut into 2-inch pieces

● Prepare a grill for barbecuing. Soak 16 thin wooden skewers in hot water. In a small nonstick skillet, heat the oil until shimmering over medium heat. Add the gingerroot and sauté 5 minutes. Let stand away from the heat 10 minutes.

● Add the soy sauce to the gingerroot and heat to boiling. Reduce heat to low and simmer, uncovered, until most of the soy sauce is absorbed, about 5 minutes. Stir in the vinegar, sugar, and sake and heat, stirring, until the sugar dissolves. Place the shrimp on a foil-lined baking sheet. Drizzle with 2 tablespoons of the gingerroot mixture and toss to coat. Double skewer the shrimp, alternating with the lime wedges skewered through the skin, the water chestnuts, and the scallions.

● Oil the grill rack. Grill shrimp over medium-high heat until bright pink and cooked through, 4 to 6 minutes, basting with remaining ginger mixture and turning every 2 minutes.

PER SERVING: 365 CALORIES; 37 G PROTEIN; 23 G CARBOHYDRATES; 14 G TOTAL FAT; 1 G SATURATED FAT; 259 MG CHOLESTEROL; 767 MG SODIUM

COOKS' TIP:

If you've never had fresh water chestnuts, you don't know what you're missing. They are so crunchy and dense that you may not recognize canned ones in comparison. Buy them in Asian markets; they keep for 7 to 10 days in the crisper if you store them in a brown paper bag.

Poultry

Hot Paprika and Marjoram • Chicken Breasts

Chicken with Honey and Sake Glaze •

Spicy Chicken Satay •

Lemongrass Chicken •

Green-Apple Martini Chicken •

Turkey Breast with • Honey-Mustard Cream Sauce

• Sweet and Sour Barbecued Chicken Thighs

• Maple-Grilled Chicken

• Arugula-Provolone Chicken Rolls with Roasted Garlic-Pepper Sauce

• Lemon-Garlic Chicken Thighs

• Chicken Veronique Brochettes

• Balsamic-Maple Duck

PREP TIME: 5 MINUTES   COOKING TIME: 15 MINUTES

Hot Paprika and Marjoram Chicken Breasts

MAKES 4 SERVINGS

The oregano-like herb called marjoram is a member of the mint family. If you can't find it fresh, you may want to grow a pot or two of it to have on hand all year, providing you can bring it into a sunny room for the winter. It's used in abundance in this recipe so that each plump chicken breast can get well seasoned with its flavor.

1/3 cup extra virgin olive oil

1/2 cup coarsely chopped marjoram leaves

1/2 cup coarsely chopped flat-leaf parsley

1 tablespoon hot paprika

kosher salt and freshly ground black pepper

4 thick boneless chicken breast halves, with the skin on (about 1/2 pound each)

● Prepare a grill and grill rack for barbecuing. In a medium bowl, mix the oil, marjoram, parsley, paprika, salt, and pepper. Rub the chicken breasts under and over the skin with the mixture.

● Grill the chicken breasts over medium-hot heat until the skin is crisp and the meat is cooked through, about 15 minutes in all, turning every 2 minutes.

PER SERVING: 426 CALORIES; 38 G PROTEIN; 2 G CARBOHYDRATES; 29 G TOTAL FAT; 4 G SATURATED FAT; 102 MG CHOLESTEROL; 238 MG SODIUM

COOKS' TIP:

If you can't find marjoram, substitute fresh oregano or mint.

PREP TIME: 25 MINUTES   COOKING TIME: 16 MINUTES

Chicken with Honey and Sake Glaze

MAKES 4 SERVINGS

Sake is more than a beer and not exactly a wine because it's made from rice, which is a grain, and not a fruit. Sake is new territory for cooks and diners because it is a clean but distinct flavor that is hard to categorize but is easy to pour and drink. Unlike tequila, sake is not cloying on the palate.

1/3 cup sake or dry sherry
1/3 cup honey
3 tablespoons roasted-garlic teriyaki sauce
4 small boneless chicken breast halves, with the
    skin on
oil for the grill

● Prepare a grill for barbecuing. Combine the sake, honey, and teriyaki sauce in a shallow baking dish and mix well. Add the chicken and turn to coat well. Marinate at least 15 minutes or cover with plastic wrap and marinate in the refrigerator 2 hours or overnight.

● Oil the grill rack. Place chicken skin side down on the grill, cover, and cook 6 inches over high heat for 16 minutes, turning and basting with marinade every 4 minutes. Remove chicken to a cutting board, cover loosely with foil, and let stand 5 minutes. Slice on the diagonal into 1/4-inch thick slices.

PER SERVING: 353 CALORIES; 30 G PROTEIN; 39 G CARBOHYDRATES; 8 G TOTAL FAT; 2 G SATURATED FAT; 82 MG CHOLESTEROL; 620 MG SODIUM

COOKS' TIP:

Ask your wine and spirits advisor to describe the different types of sake. Since so little is used in the marinade, you will want to drink the remainder, a reason to invest in a modestly priced but interesting selection.

Spicy Chicken Satay

MAKES 4 SERVINGS

It's worth a visit to an Asian market to discover the wondrous flavor of Thai sweet chili sauce. Without any further adjustments, it's a marinade, basting sauce, sauce thickener or glaze for meat, and a tasty salad dressing for juicy greens or vegetables. Here, the sauce is given some extra heat and heady fresh garlic flavor.

1/2 cup bottled Thai sweet chili sauce (nuoe cham ga)
  or 1/4 cup ketchup and 1/4 cup mild salsa
1/4 teaspoon crushed red pepper flakes
1 garlic clove, crushed through a press
11/4 pounds chicken cutlets, cut lengthwise into 12
  strips, about 11/2-inches wide
1 yellow bell pepper, seeded, cut into 8 wedges
1 red bell pepper, seeded, cut into 8 wedges
4 fat scallions, trimmed, cut crosswise into
  1-inch pieces
oil for the grill

● Prepare the grill for barbecuing. Soak eight 12-inch thin wooden skewers in hot water. Combine chili sauce, red pepper flakes, and garlic in a shallow baking dish and mix well. Add chicken strips and toss to coat. Let marinate at least 10 minutes.

● Thread chicken strips, bell pepper wedges, and scallions onto skewers, alternating ingredients. Grill skewers 6 to 8 minutes, until the chicken is cooked through, basting with marinade and turning every 2 minutes.

PER SERVING: 315 CALORIES; 43 G PROTEIN; 23 G CARBOHYDRATES; 5 G TOTAL FAT; 1 G SATURATED FAT; 114 MG CHOLESTEROL; 508 MG SODIUM

COOKS' TIP:

If you have time, you can marinate the chicken up to a day ahead of cooking.

Lemongrass Chicken

MAKES 4 SERVINGS

The woody, citrus flavored herb, lemongrass, is a staple in Thai and Vietnamese cooking. It makes a lively contribution to a garlic chive and soy-sauce marinade for plump chicken thighs. Melted butter is a Western indulgence to the basting sauce and coats the skinless chicken pieces and the lips for a sweet finish.

4 fat stalks fresh lemongrass

1/2 cup snipped garlic chives, or 1/2 cup snipped regular chives and 1 clove garlic, crushed through a press

1 tablespoon soy sauce

1 tablespoon sweet Thai chili sauce, or more to taste

4 tablespoons melted butter

8 boneless, skinless chicken thighs, scored lightly

• Prepare a grill for barbecuing. Cut off the root ends and top two-thirds of the lemongrass stalks. Remove and discard the first 2 outer layers of the bottom pieces. Coarsely chop the tender bottom third of the bulbs and place them into a food processor. Add the garlic chives or chives and garlic, soy sauce, and chili sauce; process until lemongrass and chives are evenly chopped. With machine running, add melted butter; process until smooth.

• Place chicken on foil-lined baking sheet and rub with lemongrass mixture. Grill over medium-high heat, turning every 4 to 5 minutes, until browned and cooked through, about 15 minutes in all.

PER SERVING: 332 CALORIES; 27 G PROTEIN; 3 G CARBOHYDRATES; 23 G TOTAL FAT; 10 G SATURATED FAT; 130 MG CHOLESTEROL; 72 MG SODIUM

COOKS' TIP:

Lemongrass is available in Asian grocery stores. Cut off the tops and 3 inches from the bottom root end and save for skewers or stocks, storing them in the freezer in freezer-safe plastic bags for about 6 weeks. Peel off at least 2 of the outer layers of leaves to reach the tender inner ones. Those you can chop finely and use immediately or freeze them for up to 6 weeks in a freezer-weight plastic bag or container.

PREP TIME: 25 MINUTES   COOKING TIME: 30 MINUTES

Green-Apple Martini Chicken

MAKES 4 SERVINGS

All the elements of the trendy cocktail work well to flavor chicken or even Cornish hens or veal.

1/3 cup dry white vermouth

1/3 cup extra virgin olive oil, plus extra for the grill

4 juniper berries, crushed with a rolling pin

12 pimiento-stuffed olives

2 Granny Smith apples, halved lengthwise, cored
  and quartered

4 thick boneless chicken breast halves, with the skin
  on (about 1/2 pound each)

COOKS' TIP:

If you can't find juniper berries, add 2 tablespoons gin to the marinade.

● Prepare a grill for barbecuing. Soak eight thin wooden skewers in hot water. Mix the vermouth, oil, and crushed juniper berries in a shallow baking dish. Add the olives, apples, and chicken, and toss to coat. Marinate 10 minutes.

● Oil the grill. Drain the chicken and pat dry. Skewer the olives on one skewer. Double skewer the apple quarters through the skin. Place the chicken breasts skin side down on the grill and cook, covered, with the grill vents partially closed, over high heat 4 minutes. Baste with the marinade and turn. Cover, cook 4 minutes, baste, and turn. Cover, cook 4 minutes, baste, and turn. Cover, cook 4 minutes, until white throughout when cut with knife. Remove to a serving platter, cover loosely with foil, and let rest 5 minutes.

● While the chicken rests, oil the grill again and cook the apple skewers over high heat for 1 minute on each side or until fruit is hot and tender. Remove to a plate. Heat the olives through on the grill, about 1 minute over high heat. Remove to the plate with the apples. Unthread the apples and olives around the platter with the chicken and drizzle with remaining marinade.

PER SERVING: 599 CALORIES; 41 G PROTEIN; 12 G CARBOHYDRATES;
42 G TOTAL FAT; 5 G SATURATED FAT; 114 MG CHOLESTEROL; 318 MG SODIUM

Turkey Breast with Honey-Mustard Cream Sauce

MAKES 6 SERVINGS

Thanksgiving and turkey can get boring if you have only a few people to serve, so why not grill the traditional bird for a different holiday blast?

1 skinless, boneless turkey breast half
   (about 3 1/2 pounds)
4 tablespoons butter, melted
4 tablespoons bourbon
1 teaspoon salt
1/2 teaspoon freshly ground pepper
1/2 teaspoon cinnamon
oil for the grill
1/4 cup dried cranberries
Honey-Mustard Cream Sauce, recipe follows

• Prepare a grill for barbecuing. Place the turkey breast on a foil-lined baking sheet and cut midway in half through the thickest part to about 2 inches from the end of the thin part. Open up the halves like a book and pound lightly with a meat mallet to make an even 1-inch thickness. Mix butter, bourbon, salt, pepper, and cinnamon and spread over both sides of the turkey.

• Oil the grill. Grill the turkey breast over medium-high heat 8 to 10 minutes per side or until cooked through, basting with butter mixture before turning. Place on a cutting board and cover loosely with foil. Let stand 5 minutes before slicing.

• While turkey is resting, add cranberries to the Honey-Mustard Cream Sauce and heat over medium-low heat until hot and cranberries have plumped. Slice turkey and serve with sauce.

TURKEY ONLY, PER SERVING: 510 CALORIES; 58 G PROTEIN;
1 G CARBOHYDRATE; 26 G TOTAL FAT; 10 G SATURATED FAT;
193 MG CHOLESTEROL; 619 MG SODIUM

PREP TIME: 5 MINUTES   COOKING TIME: 10 MINUTES

Honey-Mustard Cream Sauce

MAKES 6 SERVINGS, ABOUT 1²/3 CUPS

You can use prepared honey-mustard, but often a bottled blend isn't heavy enough on the honey to make the distinctive floral flavor break from the earthy mustard paste. Use pine or tupelo honey to get an assertive sweetness that "cuts the mustard."

¹/3 cup prepared Dijon or Dijon-style mustard
2 eggs
1¹/4 cups heavy cream or half-and-half
1 tablespoon honey or more to taste
1 tablespoon any kind of vinegar
¹/2 teaspoon chopped fresh dill or thyme (optional)
freshly ground pepper to taste

● In a small saucepan, combine mustard, eggs, cream, honey, and vinegar. Heat over medium-low heat, whisking constantly, until smooth. Add dill, if using, and pepper to taste. Cook, whisking, until thickened and steaming but not boiling, about 5 minutes.

PER SERVING: 110 CALORIES; 4 G PROTEIN; 7 G CARBOHYDRATES; 8 G TOTAL FAT; 4 G SATURATED FAT; 89 MG CHOLESTEROL; 196 MG SODIUM

PREP TIME: 10 MINUTES   COOKING TIME: 25 MINUTES

Sweet and Sour Barbecued Chicken Thighs

MAKES 4 SERVINGS

You can use your favorite bottled barbecue sauce instead of making one and marinate the chicken thighs in the refrigerator a day ahead of cooking.

8 chicken thighs with the skin on (about 1 1/2 pounds total)
Sweet and Sour Barbecue Sauce, recipe follows
oil for the grill
2 tablespoons chopped cilantro
1 scallion, thinly sliced

COOKS' TIP:

Skin and score the chicken thighs almost to the bone with a sharp boning knife without separating the meat from the bones. Marinate and grill.

● Prepare a grill for barbecuing. Place the chicken thighs in a large, shallow baking dish, and pour half the Sweet and Sour Barbecue Sauce over them. Turn the pieces to coat with sauce.

● Oil the grill rack. Grill the chicken, skin side down, over medium-high heat until the skin is crisp and the chicken is cooked through, about 25 minutes, basting with the sauce and turning the thighs over every 5 minutes. Transfer to a warm platter and let sit 5 minutes. Sprinkle with the cilantro and scallion and serve at once.

CHICKEN ONLY, PER SERVING: 309 CALORIES; 31 G PROTEIN;
1 G CARBOHYDRATES; 19 G TOTAL FAT; 5 G SATURATED FAT;
115 MG CHOLESTEROL; 107 MG SODIUM

PREP TIME: 5 MINUTES   COOKING TIME: 22 MINUTES

Sweet and Sour Barbecue Sauce

MAKES 4 SERVINGS, ABOUT 3/4 CUP

Bottled barbecue sauces are expensive, but who has time to make them from scratch? Here's a recipe to double and store half in the refrigerator. You'll not only save money, but you will enjoy a more "natural" sauce.

2 tablespoons butter

1 medium onion, finely chopped (about 3/4 cup)

2 tablespoons any kind of vinegar

2 tablespoons Worcestershire sauce

2 teaspoons brown sugar

1/2 teaspoon dried oregano leaves, crushed

1/4 teaspoon garlic powder or 2 small garlic cloves, crushed through a press

1/4 teaspoon freshly ground pepper

Tabasco sauce to taste

• Melt butter in a small nonstick skillet over medium heat. Add onion and sauté until softened, about 7 minutes. Add remaining ingredients and simmer 15 minutes.

PER SERVING: 66 CALORIES; 1 G PROTEIN; 6 G CARBOHYDRATES; 6 G TOTAL FAT; 4 G SATURATED FAT; 16 MG CHOLESTEROL; 72 MG SODIUM

COOKS' TIP:

The sauce is a delicious marinade for pork chops, pork tenderloin, pork loin, and chicken breasts and thighs.

PREP TIME: 5 MINUTES   COOKING TIME: 14 MINUTES

Maple-Grilled Chicken

MAKES 4 SERVINGS

Almost twice as sweet as granulated white sugar, maple sugar also has a unique flavor that comes from the concentrated sap of the maple tree. Here, the syrup, which is the middle stage between sap and sugar, glazes the skin that bastes rich dark meat chicken, and the flavor penetrates the juicy flesh for succulent eating. A mix of spices adds a heady fragrance and comfort-food taste.

4 boneless chicken breast halves (2 1/2 pounds total),
  with skin on
2 tablespoons grapeseed or canola oil plus extra for
  the grill
2 teaspoons kosher salt
1/2 teaspoon ground cloves
1/2 teaspoon ground allspice
1/4 cup maple syrup

• Prepare a grill for barbecuing. Place chicken breasts on a foil-lined baking sheet. In a small cup, mix 2 tablespoons oil with the salt, cloves, and allspice and brush over both sides of the chicken.

• Brush the grill rack with oil and grill the chicken over medium-high heat 5 minutes per side. Brush the maple syrup over the top side and turn breasts over. Grill 1 to 2 minutes, until glaze is caramelized. Brush the bottom side of breast with remaining syrup and turn over. Grill 1 to 2 minutes, until glaze is caramelized and chicken breasts are cooked through.

PER SERVING: 365 CALORIES; 30 G PROTEIN; 14 G CARBOHYDRATES;
21 G TOTAL FAT; 4 G SATURATED FAT; 93 MG CHOLESTEROL; 672 MG SODIUM

COOKS' TIP:

This seasoning mix is also nice on Cornish hens, duck, and pork.

PREP TIME: 20 MINUTES   COOKING TIME: 15 MINUTES

Arugula-Provolone Chicken Rolls with Roasted Garlic-Pepper Sauce

MAKES 4 SERVINGS

Knowledge of your grill helps to cook these dense rolls to perfection as the heat and air flow through the grill with the top down and the vents opened to control the intensity of the heat. Otherwise, without covering and venting, you could sear the outsides of the chicken rolls and the middles would be raw.

4 thin slices pancetta
4 large, thin chicken cutlets (about 1 1/2 pounds total)
8 thin slices provolone cheese
1 bunch (6 ounces) arugula, cleaned, leaves only
lemon-pepper seasoning
extra virgin olive oil for brushing
Roasted Garlic-Pepper Sauce, recipe follows

COOKS' TIPS:

• You can stuff and cook turkey or veal cutlets using the same recipe and use watercress leaves instead of arugula.

• The pancetta can also be rolled up inside of the chicken with the cheese, if you'd like.

• Prepare a grill for barbecuing. Spread out pancetta on a foil-lined baking sheet and top each slice with a cutlet, smooth side down. Place 2 slices of cheese over each piece of chicken to cover. Top with arugula leaves and sprinkle with lemon-pepper seasoning. Roll up pinwheel fashion, starting from one long side; rearrange the pancetta if necessary so it covers the roll instead of being rolled up into it. Tie the rolls at the ends and 1-inch intervals with kitchen string. Brush with olive oil and sprinkle lemon-pepper seasoning.

• Oil the grill rack and grill the rolls over medium-high heat with the grill closed and the vents partially closed, until chicken is cooked through, about 15 minutes, brushing with oil and turning rolls every 5 minutes.

• Remove the chicken rolls to a cutting board and let rest 5 minutes. Remove strings and cut into 1/2-inch-thick slices on the diagonal. Spoon a little Roasted Garlic-Pepper Sauce onto large plates and swirl with the bottom of a ladle to neatly spread it out. Transfer rolls on top of sauce so the fillings can be seen. Pass the remaining sauce.

CHICKEN ROLLS ONLY, PER SERVING: 416 CALORIES; 53 G PROTEIN; 2 G CARBOHYDRATES; 21 G TOTAL FAT; 9 G SATURATED FAT; 145 MG CHOLESTEROL; 591 MG SODIUM

PREP TIME: 10 MINUTES

Roasted Garlic-Pepper Sauce

MAKES ABOUT 8 SERVINGS, ABOUT 1 1/4 CUPS

This sauce makes a flavorful layer in a lasagna, on stuffed peppers, or a grilled beef steak or lamb chop.

2 jars (7 ounces each) roasted red peppers, drained and sliced

1 head roasted garlic (recipe, page 165)

2 tablespoons fresh lemon juice

1/2 teaspoon dried oregano or Italian seasoning

1/4 to 1/2 cup or more hot water, broth, or other liquid such as vegetable cooking water (if it's not too salty)

salt and freshly ground pepper to taste

• Place peppers in a food processor. Squeeze roasted garlic cloves from skins into the food processor and add lemon juice and oregano. Process until smooth. With machine running, pour in enough water to make sauce a coating consistency. Season with salt and pepper.

PER SERVING: 28 CALORIES; 1 G PROTEIN; 7 G CARBOHYDRATES; 2 G TOTAL FAT; 0 G SATURATED FAT; 0 MG CHOLESTEROL; 323 MG SODIUM

Lemon-Garlic Chicken Thighs

MAKES 4 SERVINGS

Pungent garlic, hot pepper, lively cilantro, and sweet lemonade make an assertive marinade that adds its charm in just a few minutes.

6 garlic cloves

1/4 cup lemonade concentrate (from frozen)

1 1/2 tablespoons cracked black pepper

1 tablespoon extra virgin olive oil, plus more for the grill

1 teaspoon kosher salt, plus more for seasoning

1 teaspoon crushed red pepper flakes

1 cup cilantro leaves

8 boneless chicken thighs, with skin on (about 5 ounces each)

1/2 cup fresh salsa, for serving

lemon wedges, for serving

● Prepare a grill for barbecuing. In a blender or food processor, process the garlic with the lemonade concentrate, pepper, 1 tablespoon oil, the salt, and red pepper flakes until smooth. Add the cilantro and process until a chunky paste forms. Place the chicken on a foil-lined baking sheet and rub the garlic paste under the skin and all over the chicken thighs. Let the chicken stand at room temperature for 10 minutes.

● Brush the grill rack with oil and grill the chicken skin side up for 6 minutes. Turn and grill for 6 minutes longer, until the skin is crisp and the chicken is cooked through. Transfer the chicken to plates and serve with the salsa and lemon wedges.

PER SERVING: 505 CALORIES; 34 G PROTEIN; 19 G CARBOHYDRATES; 32 G TOTAL FAT; 9 G SATURATED FAT; 158 MG CHOLESTEROL; 875 G SODIUM

Chicken Veronique Brochettes

MAKES 4 SERVINGS

The classic seedless white grape garnish called Veronique is given a new interpretation here as a colorful mix of grapes are skewered alongside shallots and cubes of chicken. Served with a vermouth-spiked gravy, the flavors are both homey and fancy.

1¹/2 *pounds boneless, skinless chicken cutlets, cut into 1-inch cubes*

12 shallot lobes, peeled, quartered lengthwise through the root

12 seedless red grapes

12 seedless black grapes

12 seedless green grapes

2 tablespoons vegetable oil, plus more for the grill

2 tablespoons soy sauce

1 cup chicken gravy (homemade or prepared)

1/2 cup dry white vermouth

1 teaspoon chopped fresh thyme leaves

- Prepare a grill for barbecuing. Soak 12 bamboo skewers in hot water.

- Double thread the chicken cubes, shallots, and grapes onto the skewers, alternating the pieces, and skewering the shallots first through the widest side of the wedges. Place the skewers on a foil-lined baking sheet. Mix 2 tablespoons oil and the soy sauce in a small bowl and brush the mixture over the brochettes.

- Brush the grill with oil. Grill the brochettes 6 inches from medium-hot coals, 12 to 15 minutes or until the chicken and shallots are tender, turning the brochettes every 3 minutes, and brushing with remaining oil-soy sauce mixture.

- While brochettes cook, mix gravy with vermouth and thyme in a microwave-safe bowl. Microwave, covered, on HIGH power, 2 mintues or until hot, or in a saucepan over medium-high heat until boiling. Serve the gravy mixture with the brochettes.

PER SERVING: 452 CALORIES; 46 G PROTEIN; 27 G CARBOHYDRATES; 16 G TOTAL FAT; 3 G SATURATED FAT; 117 MG CHOLESTEROL; 973 MG SODIUM

Balsamic-Maple Duck

MAKES 4 SERVINGS

Steaming the duck before grilling not only does most of the cooking, but it removes enough of the fat from under the skin so that it grills without causing a fire in the coals. Here, the time the duck spends on the grill is used to sear the skin to give it an appetizing look and crispness.

4 boneless duck or chicken breast halves with the
  skin on
1 teaspoon salt
2 tablespoons balsamic vinegar
2 tablespoons pure maple syrup
oil for the grill

● Place duck breasts skin side up on a heat-safe dish and sprinkle with 1 scant teaspoon of salt. Let stand at least 15 minutes or cover with plastic wrap and refrigerate for 2 hours or overnight.

● Prepare a grill for barbecuing and a steamer for cooking. Mix the vinegar and syrup in a cup and brush the mixture over the duck. Steam, in 2 batches if necessary, for 7 minutes.

● Carefully remove the duck from the steamer. Oil the grill rack and grill the duck skin side down over high heat, 3 inches from heat source, for 2 minutes. Cool to room temperature. Cut breasts into 1/4-inch slices and serve.

PER SERVING: 512 CALORIES; 59 G PROTEIN; 7 G CARBOHYDRATES; 26 G TOTAL FAT; 7 G SATURATED FAT; 326 MG CHOLESTEROL; 780 MG SODIUM

Meats

Pepper-Glazed Rib-Eyes with Grilled Watercress

Fontina Fonduta Burgers

Teriyaki Steak Wraps

Grilled Citrus Flank Steak

Stuffed Mini-Meat Loaves

Jack Cheese Steak Burritos

Beef and Eggplant Shashlik

Grilled Steaks Rossini

Beef Tenderloin with Olive Relish

Veal Chops with Thyme and Honey

Veal Kebabs with Grapes and Mint

Veal Cutlets with Arugula Salad and Quick Preserved Lemons

Veal Confetti Burgers

Veal Tenderloins with Anchovy-Caper Butter

Lamb Steaks with Spiced Dried Fruit and Agrodolce Sauce

Grilled Lamb Chops with Pink Peppercorn Sauce

Harmon Steak-Spinach Pinwheels

Lamb Skewers with Lemons and Red Onions

Feta-Lamb Kebabs with Yogurt Sauce

Fruit and Nut Lamb Burgers

Lamb Chops with Spicy Thai Peanut Sauce

Curried Honey-Mustard Lamb Loin

Spiced Lamb Chops

Lamb Teriyaki with Mushrooms

Mustard-Crusted Lamb Rack

Lamb Chops with Fennel and Parmigiano Reggiano Butter

Provençal Burgers

Pork Tenderloins with Syrah-Date Sauce

Chili-Brine Pork Chops with Tasty Fresh Salsa

Taco'd Pork Kebabs

Pork with Green Curry Sauce and Grilled Mango

Grilled-Arugula and Prosciutto Calzones

Seared Pork and Pickled Pepper Panini

Pork Chops with Pomegranate Glaze

Pork Medallions with Orange-Chile Sauce

Grilled-Portobello and Pancetta Soup

PREP TIME: 25 MINUTES   COOKING TIME: 14 MINUTES

Pepper-Glazed Rib-Eyes with Grilled Watercress

MAKES 4 SERVINGS

You don't need to do a lot of razzle-dazzle to rib-eye steaks; they are A-list stars of the grill without any fanfare. Because thick steaks cook more easily and better than thin ones, it's best to either split one between 2 people or to splurge and have one for each person.

2 rib-eye steaks (10 to 12 ounces each),
    cut 1-inch thick
2 tablespoons extra virgin olive oil, plus extra
    for the grill
1 tablespoon lemon-pepper seasoning
1 tablespoon Worcestershire sauce
salt
1 bunch watercress, stemmed, rinsed, drained
1 tablespoon grapeseed oil

• Brush the steaks on both sides with some of the olive oil and rub with the lemon-pepper seasoning. In a small bowl, mix the remaining olive oil with the Worcestershire sauce.

• Prepare a grill for barbecuing. Grill the steaks over medium-high heat for 8 minutes. Brush each side with half the olive-oil mixture and grill 1 minute on each side for medium-rare meat. Transfer the steaks to a cutting board, sprinkle with salt, and let rest for 5 minutes.

• Meanwhile, grease a vegetable basket and place on the grill. In a large bowl, drizzle the watercress with the grapeseed oil and sprinkle with salt. Toss to coat. Place in the vegetable basket, cover the grill and cook the watercress 2 minutes. Stir and cook until wilted, about 2 minutes longer. Remove to a warm platter. Sprinkle with the remaining Worcestershire mixture and toss.

• Cut the steak across the grain in $1/4$-inch-thick slices. Arrange the meat on the watercress and pour any meat juices over the steaks.

PER SERVING: 301 CALORIES; 29 G PROTEIN; 2 G CARBOHYDRATES; 20 G TOTAL FAT; 5 G SATURATED FAT; 686 MG CHOLESTEROL; 925 MG SODIUM

PREP TIME: 20 MINUTES   COOKING TIME: 15 MINUTES

Fontina Fonduta Burgers

MAKES 4 SERVINGS

Fontina is one of Italy's (and the world's) great cheeses, so even if you love the mild domestic version, you will want to use the real thing here in the sauce for the bunless burger—you will really taste the difference.

1/4 cup plus 2 tablespoons dry white wine

7 ounces imported Fontina cheese, cut into 1/4-inch pieces (1 1/4 cups)

3/4 pound ground sirloin, at room temperature

3/4 pound ground chuck, at room temperature

salt and freshly ground pepper

vegetable oil, for brushing

4 Boston lettuce leaves

1/4 cup mixed finely chopped green, red, yellow, and purple bell peppers

COOKS' TIP:

Fonduta, or dish of melted cheese, is the Italian version of "fondue" and can be used as a dip for bread or blanched vegetables.

• Prepare a grill for barbecuing. In a small saucepan, warm the wine over medium heat. Add the cheese and cook over low heat, stirring with a wooden spoon, until the cheese melts and the sauce is smooth. Keep warm over low heat.

• In a medium bowl, lightly knead the sirloin with the chuck and loosely form into 4 patties about 3/4-inch thick. Season the burgers very generously with salt and pepper and place on a foil-lined baking sheet.

• When the fire is medium hot, oil the grate. Grill the burgers for about 10 minutes, turning once, for medium doneness.

• Reheat sauce until it is piping hot. Set a lettuce leaf on each of four plates. Top each with a burger and a generous spoonful of cheese sauce. Sprinkle each with one-fourth of the peppers. Serve, passing the remaining cheese sauce on the side.

PER SERVING: 487 CALORIES; 33 G PROTEIN; 2 G CARBOHYDRATES; 37 G TOTAL FAT; 20 G SATURATED FAT; 148 MG CHOLESTEROL; 745 MG SODIUM

PREP TIME: 35 MINUTES   COOKING TIME: 4 MINUTES

Teriyaki Steak Wraps

MAKES 6 SERVINGS

Miso is a thick, fermented, nutritious soybean paste and is a basic flavoring in Japanese cooking. There are many textures, flavors, and colors of miso, and many are used for specific dishes. You can find miso in Japanese grocery stores and health food stores. Shinshu miso is a golden, mellow flavored, all-purpose variety that works well in this marinade. Use it in salad dressings, soups, dips, sauces, and as a condiment. Store it, tightly covered, in the refrigerator.

1 tablespoon Japanese miso

3 tablespoons mirin (sweet rice wine) or sherry

2 tablespoons low-sodium soy sauce

1 tablespoon distilled white vinegar

1 tablespoon sugar

2 teaspoons Asian sesame oil

2 pounds skirt steak, cut into 4-inch pieces

salt and freshly ground black pepper

6 round, thin mountain breads or flour tortillas,
*   (9 inches in diameter) warmed*

SAKE-SCALLION SAUCE

1 bunch scallions, trimmed, thinly sliced

1 cup sake

3 tablespoons dry sherry

2 tablespoons low-sodium soy sauce

2 teaspoons grated peeled fresh gingerroot

• Combine miso, mirin, soy sauce, vinegar, sugar, and sesame oil. Place beef in self sealing plastic bag; add marinade, seal and turn bag, and massage to coat. Let stand for 15 minutes at room temperature, or overnight in the refrigerator.

• Prepare Sake Scallion Sauce: Place all ingredients into a saucepan and bring to a boil. Lower heat and simmer into a light syrupy consistency. Set aside.

• Prepare a grill for barbecuing. Remove the steak from the marinade; season with salt and pepper. Grill over moderately high heat, turning once, until medium rare, about 4 minutes. Transfer to a cutting board; let stand for 3 minutes.

• Thinly slice the steak across the grain and place in a bowl. Pour the sauce on top and toss to coat. Drain and place equal amounts of steak in the center of each tortilla.

• Fold up the bottom and roll the tortillas into an eat-from-the-top-end cylinder.

PER SERVING: 517 CALORIES; 38 G PROTEIN; 36 G CARBOHYDRATES; 18 G TOTAL FAT; 7 G SATURATED FAT; 81 MG CHOLESTEROL; 867 MG SODIUM

PREP TIME: 20 MINUTES   COOKING TIME: 10 MINUTES

Grilled Citrus Flank Steak

MAKES 4 SERVINGS

Five-spice powder is a popular Chinese flavoring that consists of equal parts of ground cinnamon, cloves, fennel seed, star anise, and Szechuan peppercorns. You can find the mix in grocery stores or more economically in Chinese grocery stores.

1 large garlic clove, crushed through a press

1 tablespoon grated orange zest

2 tablespoons fresh lime juice

1 1/2 teaspoons salt

1 teaspoon five-spice powder

2 tablespoons olive oil, plus extra for the grill

1 flank steak (about 1 1/2 pounds)

8 lime wedges

4 orange wedges

- In a food processor, process the garlic with the orange zest, lime juice, salt, and spice powder. With the machine running, slowly drizzle the olive oil into the garlic mixture until a wet paste forms. Rub the paste all over the steak.

- Prepare a grill for barbecuing. Oil the grill and grill the steak over a medium-high heat for 10 minutes, turning once, until an instant-read thermometer inserted in the thickest part registers 125° to 130° F for medium rare. Transfer the steak to a cutting board and let rest for 5 minutes.

- Cut the steak across the grain into 1/4-inch-thick slices. Arrange the meat on a platter with the lime and orange wedges.

PER SERVING: 310 CALORIES; 27 G PROTEIN; 1 G CARBOHYDRATES; 22 G TOTAL FAT; 7 G SATURATED FAT; 71 MG CHOLESTEROL; 963 MG SODIUM

COOKS' TIP:

You can use pork tenderloin, chicken parts, duck breasts, or Cornish hens instead of beef in this recipe.

Stuffed Mini-Meat Loaves

MAKES 8 PATTIES

Here, one of the cornerstones of comfort food takes to the grill as easily as it does to church-basement suppers.

2 pounds lean ground beef

1 envelope French onion soup mix

1 jar (5 ounces) chopped pimientos, drained,
*   or 1/2 cup chopped homemade or jarred roasted*
*   red peppers*

1 cup cornbread stuffing mix

1/2 cup of either tomato juice, mixed-vegetable juice,
*   Bloody Mary mix, chicken broth, or water*

1 cup shredded cheese (Cheddar, Jack, mozzarella,
*   or other kind, or a mix of remnants)*

vegetable oil for the grill

COOKS' TIP:

You can substitute a mixture of beef, pork, and veal for the all-beef version, or use ground turkey or chicken (a mixture of dark and light meats). Test the loaves with an instant-read thermometer to make sure the centers are cooked to 179° F.

● Prepare a grill for barbecuing. In a large bowl, combine the beef and soup mix and gently mix. In another bowl, combine the pimientos, stuffing mix, tomato juice, and cheese. Divide the beef mixture into 8 oval patties and make an oval dent in the centers with your thumb. Fill the dents of four of the patties with one-fourth of the pimiento mixture and top each with a remaining patty, dent side down. Press edges to seal. Place meat loaves on a foil-lined baking sheet. (If desired, cover with plastic wrap and refrigerate up to 8 hours before grilling; allow meat loaves to sit at room temperature about 30 minutes before grilling. Prepare grill when loaves leave the fridge.)

● Brush the grill rack with oil. Grill meat loaves 6 inches from medium-hot coals 10 minutes, turning after 5 minutes for medium-rare meat loaves.

PER PATTY: 320 CALORIES; 26 G PROTEIN; 10 G CARBOHYDRATES; 19 G TOTAL FAT; 9 G SATURATED FAT; 86 MG CHOLESTEROL; 716 MG SODIUM

Jack Cheese Steak Burritos

MAKES 6 SERVINGS

Be sure to slice the meat as thinly as possible — 1/4 inch is the max — for maximum tenderness. The meat will be easier to cut if you freeze it slightly.

1 bottom round or rump roast (about 2 1/2 pounds)

2 tablespoons roasted-garlic teriyaki sauce

4 tablespoons grapeseed or extra virgin olive oil

2 red onions

salt

8 lime wedges

1 cup shredded Monterey Jack cheese with
    jalapeños, shredded

2 tablespoons chopped cilantro

6 corn tortillas (6 inches in diameter), warmed

• Prepare a grill for barbecue. Slice roast across grain into 1/4-inch-thick slices and place in a medium bowl. Add the teriyaki sauce and 2 tablespoons of the oil and toss to coat. Let stand for 15 minutes at room temperature or overnight in the refrigerator.

• Peel the onions and cut into 1/4-inch-thick wedges through the root so the layers stay together. Place in another medium bowl and drizzle with the remaining 2 tablespoons oil. Sprinkle with salt and toss to coat.

• Remove meat from marinade; wipe off excess. Place onions in an oiled, hinged wire basket. Grill over hot coals until tender, turning basket every 2 minutes, about 8 minutes in all. When onions have been cooking about 5 minutes, grill meat slices alongside onions, 1 to 1 1/2 minutes on each side, or until seared.

• To serve: Place beef slices on a platter, top with the onions, and sprinkle with salt. Squeeze 2 lime wedges over all, then top with the shredded cheese and cilantro. Serve with the warm corn tortillas and the remaining lime wedges.

PER SERVING: 585 CALORIES; 44 G PROTEIN; 18 G CARBOHYDRATES; 37 G TOTAL FAT; 12 G SATURATED FAT; 129 MG CHOLESTEROL; 477 MG SODIUM

COOKS' TIP:

You can increase the amount of cheese if you like more than a sprinkle.

PREP TIME: 40 MINUTES   COOKING TIME: 10 MINUTES

Beef and Eggplant Shashlik

MAKES 4 SERVINGS

Russians use long metal skewers for their kebabs, but if you don't have them, bamboo ones will do. Serve the kebabs with grated raw onion for an authentic Slavic touch.

1/2 cup bottled garlic vinaigrette dressing

2 teaspoons ground coriander

1 1/2 pounds well trimmed boneless sirloin steak, cut into 3/4-inch cubes

1 red onion, peeled and cut lengthwise into 3/4-inch wedges, layers separated

2 small Japanese eggplants, cut crosswise into 1/2-inch rounds

• Mix the dressing and coriander in a shallow glass baking dish. Add the steak cubes, onion, and eggplant and toss to coat. Cover with plastic wrap and marinate at least 15 minutes at room temperature or refrigerate up to 24 hours, stirring occasionally.

• Prepare a grill for barbecuing. Soak wooden or bamboo skewers in hot water 15 minutes. Thread beef, onion, and eggplant pieces in an alternate arrangement onto the skewers; reserve marinade. Grease the grill rack and cook the skewers over medium-high heat 6 to 10 minutes, turning frequently and basting with the reserved marinade, until cooked to desired doneness.

PER SERVING: 528 CALORIES; 40 G PROTEIN; 12 G CARBOHYDRATES; 35 G TOTAL FAT; 11 G SATURATED FAT; 122 MG CHOLESTEROL; 321 MG SODIUM

COOKS' TIP:

Stop basting the last 2 minutes of cooking so the meat juices in the marinade on the kebabs will be cooked thoroughly.

PREP TIME: 20 MINUTES   COOKING TIME: 15 MINUTES

Grilled Steaks Rossini

MAKES 4 SERVINGS

This classic showstopper is named after the universally honored Italian gourmand and composer of *The Barber of Seville*. It is served on a round of toast so that every drop of the meat juices can be enjoyed.

4 beef tenderloin steaks, tied (about 6 ounces each)

1 tablespoon grapeseed oil or extra virgin olive oil

kosher salt and freshly ground pepper

1 container (8 ounces) prepared goose, chicken, or
*   duck liver mousse with truffles*

4 crustless rounds country-style Italian bread,
*   the size of the steaks*

2 tablespoons beef demi-glace (sauce made from
*   reduced stock)*

1 cup salt-free or low-sodium beef stock or water

- Prepare a grill for barbecuing. Rub steaks on both sides with oil, and sprinkle with salt and pepper. Remove mousse from container and place on sheet of plastic wrap. Divide the mousse into 4 equal parts. Roll each section into a round the size of the steak. Chill briefly in freezer. (This can all be done ahead and refrigerated until ready to cook.)

- Grill the steaks over medium-high heat, turning once, about 15 minutes in all for medium-rare meat. Top each steak with a round of mousse during the last 2 minutes of cooking to heat the mousse, but not long enough to melt it. Transfer the steaks to a warm platter and loosely cover with foil. Let stand for 5 minutes.

- While steaks set, toast breads and heat demi-glace with stock to boiling; keep warm. When steaks have set, remove the strings, place toasts on plates, and top with steaks. Keep warm. Pour sauce around steaks— you may have extra sauce remaining.

PER SERVING: 523 CALORIES; 34 G PROTEIN; 24 G CARBOHYDRATES; 31 G TOTAL FAT; 10 G SATURATED FAT; 133 MG CHOLESTEROL; 604 MG SODIUM

COOKS' TIP:

Demi-glace is available in gourmet food shops, and usually it is frozen. If you can't find it, whisk a tablespoon of soft unsalted butter into the hot stock until the butter is barely melted. Do not boil the mixture at this point or the butter will lose its thickening power and simply melt.

Beef Tenderloin with Olive Relish

MAKES 8 SERVINGS

This is a basic recipe for grilling a tenderloin; it is such a deluxe piece of meat that you don't have to do more than focus on cooking it to perfection.

1 trimmed beef tenderloin (about 3 pounds)
1 tablespoon extra virgin olive oil plus extra
  for the grill
salt and freshly ground pepper
1 jar (9 3/4 ounces) olive salad
1 shallot, minced
1 tablespoon chopped fresh oregano or 1 teaspoon
  dried oregano
1 tablespoon balsamic vinegar

• Prepare a grill for barbecuing. Grease a grill rack. Fold the thin tail under the tenderloin and tie the whole tenderloin at 3/4-inch intervals with cotton kitchen string to create a uniform thickness for even grilling. Rub the tenderloin with olive oil, salt, and pepper, and grill 6 inches from medium-high heat for 20 minutes, brushing with oil and turning every 5 minutes, until tenderloin reaches an internal temperature of 145° F for medium rare.

• Remove from the grill and let rest on a cutting board for 10 minutes.

• Drain and rinse olive salad; chop finely and place in a medium bowl. Add the shallot, oregano, and vinegar and mix well.

• Slice the tenderloin on an angle and arrange on a platter. Serve with the sauce.

PER SERVING: 334 CALORIES; 39 G PROTEIN; 2 G CARBOHYDRATES; 18 G TOTAL FAT; 5 G SATURATED FAT; 114 MG CHOLESTEROL; 446 MG SODIUM

COOKS' TIP:

You can brush the tenderloin with your favorite Italian dressing instead of plain olive oil.

Veal Chops with Thyme and Honey

MAKES 6 SERVINGS

Thyme and honey combine to create succulent veal chops.

1/2 cup extra virgin olive oil

1/4 cup fresh lemon juice

1 tablepoon finely chopped fresh thyme leaves
   (no stems)

4 veal rib chops (8 ounces each), cut about
   3/4-inch thick

salt and freshly ground pepper

3 tablespoons honey

• Prepare a grill for barbecuing. In a shallow glass or other nonreactive baking dish, mix the olive oil, 2 tablespoons lemon juice, and thyme. Season the veal chops with salt and pepper. Add to the thyme mixture and turn to coat. Let stand 15 minutes, turning once. Meanwhile, mix the remaining lemon juice and the honey.

• Grill the chops over medium-hot heat until cooked to taste, 5 minutes per side for medium (barely pink inside), rotating 90 degrees after 3 minutes to make a grid of grill marks. Brush with the honey mixture the last minute of cooking on each side.

• Transfer the chops to a platter, cover loosely with foil, and let rest for 3 minutes.

PER SERVING: 402 CALORIES; 29 G PROTEIN; 10 G CARBOHYDRATES;
27 G TOTAL FAT; 4 G SATURATED FAT; 130 MG CHOLESTEROL; 303 MG SODIUM

Veal Kebabs with Grapes and Mint

MAKES 4 SERVINGS

Be sure to shake the bottle of dressing before you measure so the seasonings at the bottom will be included. You can use homemade dressing if your recipe includes garlic and herbs.

2 pounds veal loin, cut into 1-inch cubes

8 ounces seedless red grapes

8 ounces seedless green grapes

1/2 cup bottled balsamic vinaigrette

1 cup big mint leaves

kosher salt and freshly ground pepper

• Prepare grill for barbecuing. Mix veal and grapes with the dressing in a large bowl. Thread pieces alternately on skewers with mint leaves and place on foil-lined baking sheets; reserve dressing. Sprinkle with salt and pepper. Grill over medium-hot heat 8 minutes, turning every 2 minutes and brushing with reserved dressing the first 6 minutes of cooking.

PER SERVING: 512 CALORIES; 36 G PROTEIN; 23 G CARBOHYDRATES;
31 G TOTAL FAT; 9 G SATURATED FAT; 143 MG CHOLESTEROL; 388 MG SODIUM

COOKS' TIP:

You can marinate the veal by itself in the refrigerator for 1 or 2 days ahead of cooking. Stir the meat occasionally.

Veal Cutlets with Arugula Salad and Quick Preserved Lemons

MAKES 4 SERVINGS

Since they aren't coated with the traditional egg-and-crumb mixture and fried, the cutlets need to be coddled so they won't dry out or toughen. Cook them just long enough to sear the outside; they will finish cooking as they rest.

2 cups water

1/3 cup sugar

salt and freshly ground pepper

1 large lemon, very thinly sliced into 8 nice slices (without the ends), seeds removed

1/2 teaspoon dried oregano leaves

1/4 cup extra virgin olive oil

4 veal cutlets (1/2-inch thick)

1 bunch (about 6 ounces) arugula, washed, dried, stems removed and leaves torn

1/4 cup pitted cured black olives

1/4 cup halved pear tomatoes (a mixture of red and yellow, if available)

1 tablespoon fresh lemon juice

chunk of Parmigiano Reggiano cheese for serving

COOKS' TIP:

Sprinkle the dish with capers or chopped marinated sun-dried tomatoes if you like.

• Prepare a grill for barbecuing. In a small saucepan, combine the water, sugar, 1 1/2 teaspoons salt, and 1/2 teaspoon pepper and heat to boiling, stirring until the sugar and salt dissolve. Stir in the lemon slices and oregano and simmer over medium heat until lemon rind is tender, about 15 minutes. Remove the lemon slices and set aside in a bowl. Boil the liquid until it is reduced to 2 tablespoons, stir in 1/4 cup oil, and set aside.

• Arrange cutlets on a foil-lined baking sheet. Brush on both sides with lemon-oil mixture. Set aside.

• Combine arugula, olives, and tomatoes in a large bowl. Toss to mix and set aside.

• Grill cutlets over medium-high heat until barely cooked through, about 2 minutes on each side. Place on a platter and cover with foil to keep warm.

• Drizzle 2 tablespoons of the remaining lemon-oil mixture and the lemon juice over the arugula mixture and sprinkle with salt and pepper. Toss to coat. Place a cutlet on each of 4 serving plates and top with the arugula salad and 2 lemon slices. Shave some Parmigiano Reggiano on top using a cheese plane or vegetable peeler.

PER SERVING: 481 CALORIES; 51 G PROTEIN; 18 G CARBOHYDRATES; 22 G TOTAL FAT; 4 G SATURATED FAT; 179 MG CHOLESTEROL; 864 MG SODIUM

Veal Confetti Burgers

MAKES 4 SERVINGS

You can make the mix a day ahead of shaping and cooking the patties and store, covered, in the refrigerator. Let stand about 20 minutes at room temperature before grilling so the centers of the burgers will be thoroughly done.

3/4 pound ground veal

1/4 pound ground pork

1 large egg, lightly beaten

1/3 cup toasted pine nuts, coarsely chopped

1/3 cup dry white vermouth

1/4 cup diced feta cheese

1/4 cup chopped, mixed green and black olives, pitted

1/4 cup snipped fresh chives

2 tablespoons Italian-seasoned dry bread crumbs

2 tablespoons chopped marinated sun-dried tomatoes

1/2 teaspoon salt

1/4 teaspoon freshly ground pepper

1/2 teaspoon sage

extra virgin olive oil for the grill

● Prepare a grill for barbecuing. In a bowl, combine the veal, pork, egg, pine nuts, vermouth, cheese, olives, chives, bread crumbs, tomatoes, salt, pepper, and sage. Mix with your hands until combined. Shape into 4 patties, 3/4-inch thick.

● Brush the grill grate with oil. Grill burgers over high heat, turning once with a spatula, until browned on both sides and cooked through, about 4 minutes on each side.

PER SERVING: 433 CALORIES; 30 PROTEIN; 7 G CARBOHYDRATES; 30 G TOTAL FAT; 10 G SATURATED FAT; 166 MG CHOLESTEROL; 624 MG SODIUM

COOKS' TIP:
You can use finely chopped scallions instead of chives.

Veal Tenderloins with Anchovy-Caper Butter

MAKES 4 SERVINGS

If you are anchovyphobic, just about any fresh juice or saucy element will gild this prestigious piece of meat. "Merely" serving the veal with wedges of Key limes, Meyer lemons, and/or blood oranges with white-truffle oil will dazzle your guests!

2 veal tenderloins (about 1 pound each), tied
2 tablespoons olive oil
1 teaspoon dried oregano leaves
1/4 teaspoon garlic powder
kosher salt and freshly ground pepper
Anchovy-Caper Butter, recipe follows

• Prepare a grill for barbecuing. On a foil-lined baking sheet, brush the tenderloins with oil and sprinkle with oregano, garlic powder, salt, and pepper. Rub seasonings into the meat. Grill over a hot fire 8 minutes, turning every 2 minutes; move tenderloins to a medium-hot portion of the grill and cook 4 minutes longer, turning every 2 minutes. Remove to a warm platter; cover loosely with foil and let stand 5 minutes.

• Place tenderloins on a cutting board and slice into 1/4-inch slices. Serve with Anchovy-Caper Butter.

VEAL ONLY, PER SERVING: 275 CALORIES; 37 G PROTEIN; 1 G CARBOHYDRATES; 13 G TOTAL FAT; 2 G SATURATED FAT; 145 MG CHOLESTEROL; 454 MG SODIUM

Anchovy-Caper Butter

MAKES 4 SERVINGS

This tasty topping is delicious on lamb chops, spread on toast for accompanying soup, and is a nice addition to a deviled-egg filling.

8 large anchovy fillets
4 tablespoons unsalted butter, softened
2 teaspoons fresh lemon juice
1 tablespoon small capers, drained if pickled,
*   and rinsed if salted*
freshly ground pepper

• Mash anchovies and butter in a small bowl with a fork to purée the anchovies. Stir in lemon juice. Gently stir in capers and season with pepper. Set aside.

PER SERVING: 120 CALORIES; 3 G PROTEIN; 0 G CARBOHYDRATES; 12 G TOTAL FAT; 7 G SATURATED FAT; 38 MG CHOLESTEROL; 359 MG SODIUM

COOKS' TIP:

Garnish the dish with fresh thyme sprigs—stems and all.

PREP TIME: 10 MINUTES   COOKING TIME: 8 MINUTES

Lamb Steaks with Spiced Dried Fruit and Agrodolce Sauce

MAKES 4 SERVINGS

There is enough fat within the meat to baste it evenly while cooking the steaks. The sauce is nice with other cuts of lamb, from patties to chops to cubes cut for kebabs.

extra virgin olive oil
4 bone-in lamb leg steaks, 1/2- to 3/4-inch thick
    (7 to 8 ounces each)
salt and freshly ground pepper
Spiced Dried Fruit and Agrodolce Sauce,
    recipe follows

• Prepare a grill for barbecuing. Oil the grill rack. Place the lamb chops on a foil-lined baking sheet and brush on both sides with oil. Season generously on both sides with salt and pepper.

• Grill the steaks over medium-high heat, until browned, turning once, about 8 minutes in all for medium rare. Transfer the steaks to a warm platter, top with the Spiced Dried Fruit and Agrodolce Sauce and serve.

LAMB ONLY, PER SERVING: 393 CALORIES; 32 G PROTEIN; 0 G CARBOHYDRATES; 29 G TOTAL FAT; 11 G SATURATED FAT; 122 MG CHOLESTEROL; 376 MG SODIUM

COOKS' TIP:

You can use lemon-pepper seasoning or dried oregano to season the lamb if you wish.

PREP TIME: 5 MINUTES   COOKING TIME: 5 MINUTES

Spiced Dried Fruit and Agrodolce Sauce

MAKES 4 SERVINGS

Agrodolce is the Italian term for a sour and sweet flavor (agro, sour; dolce, sweet). The type of vinegar you choose will dictate how much of it you use to balance the sweetness of the fruit and honey. After your first tasting, add more drop by drop until the sauce is to your liking.

1 cup hot water
1/2 cup chopped dried fruit
6 tablespoons honey
2 bay leaves
2 tablespoons grated peeled fresh gingerroot
    (use a microplane grater)
2 to 4 tablespoons vinegar (any kind)
salt and freshly ground pepper to taste

• Combine the water, dried fruit, honey, bay leaves, and gingerroot in a small saucepan and simmer over low heat 5 minutes. Stir in 2 tablespoons vinegar and season with salt and pepper. Taste; add more vinegar according to taste. Remove bay leaves before serving.

PER SERVING: 151 CALORIES; 1 G PROTEIN; 41 G CARBOHYDRATES; 0 G TOTAL FAT; 0 MG CHOLESTEROL; 150 MG SODIUM

COOKS' TIP:

You can use a mixture of dried fruit or all of one kind. Dried currants, cranberries, apricots, and pears make a nice blend.

PREP TIME: 10 MINUTES   COOKING TIME: 7 MINUTES

Grilled Lamb Chops with Pink Peppercorn Sauce

MAKES 4 SERVINGS

As with grilling all lamb, baby chops need to be seared so the meat surface is appetizingly browned and the fat is rendered—any flabby white bits harden quickly as they cool and are not good. (Always heat your serving platter so this won't happen to any lamb you serve.) Make sure your grill rack is close enough to the heat to get the job done without overcooking the meat. Have a cool spot on the grill where there are no coals underneath so you can move the chops to safety but where they will stay warm.

extra virgin olive oil
12 baby lamb rib chops (4 ounces each)
salt and freshly ground pepper
Pink Peppercorn Sauce, recipe follows

● Prepare a grill for barbecuing. Oil the grill rack. Place the lamb chops on a foil-lined baking sheet and brush on both sides with oil. Season generously on both sides with salt and pepper.

● Grill the lamb chops over high heat, turning them once, until browned all over, about 7 minutes in all for medium-rare meat. Transfer the lamb chops to a warm serving platter, dollop the Pink Peppercorn Sauce on top, and serve.

LAMB ONLY, PER SERVING: 645 CALORIES; 38 G PROTEIN; 0 G CARBOHYDRATES; 54 G TOTAL FAT; 22 G SATURATED FAT; 168 MG CHOLESTEROL; 418 MG SODIUM

PREP TIME: 5 MINUTES

Pink Peppercorn Sauce

MAKES 4 SERVINGS

As berries in the rose family, pink peppercorns are not related to the black, white, and green berries of the pepper plant. A further distinction is that the slightly sweet pink spice is native to Madagascar, not India and Indonesia, as are the true peppercorns.

1 cup crème fraîche
3 tablespoons drained prepared horseradish
*   with beets*
2 teaspoons crushed pink peppercorns
kosher salt to taste

● In a medium bowl, mix the crème fraîche, horseradish, and peppercorns until blended. Season with salt.

PER SERVING: 112 CALORIES; 2 G PROTEIN; 4 G CARBOHYDRATES; 10 G TOTAL FAT; 6 G SATURATED FAT; 21 MG CHOLESTEROL; 206 MG SODIUM

COOKS' TIP:

Spoon a dramatic dollop of the sauce onto grilled beef steaks or roasts or to spice up baked potatoes.

PREP TIME: 30 MINUTES   COOKING TIME: 20 MINUTES

Harmon Steak-Spinach Pinwheels

MAKES 4 SERVINGS

The best choice for busy cooks is to marinate the meat in the refrigerator for 48 hours. If you want to soak and go, that's fine, too, as the marinade flavors well as a glaze. Try the marinade with beef short ribs, when you have time to cook them slowly.

MARINADE

1/2 cup soy sauce

1/4 cup sugar

2 tablespoons Asian sesame oil

4 fat scallions, trimmed, finely chopped

1 large garlic clove, crushed through a press

2 tablespoons grated peeled fresh gingerroot

PINWHEEL STEAKS

1 flank steak (2 pounds)

2 tablespoons olive oil

1 large garlic clove, crushed through a press

1 teaspoon salt

1/2 teaspoon crushed red pepper flakes

1 bag (1 pound) washed baby spinach

● Combine marinade ingredients in a small saucepan and heat to boiling, stirring to dissolve the sugar. Pour marinade into a heat-safe shallow glass baking dish and let cool to room temperature.

● Add steak to marinade. Turn to coat; marinate 10 minutes at room temperature or up to 48 hours in the refrigerator, covered with plastic wrap.

● While meat marinates, heat oil, garlic, salt, and pepper flakes in a large skillet over medium-high heat until fragrant. Add spinach and stir-fry until wilted. Remove from heat.

● Prepare a grill for barbecuing. Drain the marinade into a saucepan. Meanwhile, place the steak between 2 sheets of waxed paper. Pound with a rolling pin to an even thickness. Remove the waxed paper and spread the spinach mixture on top but leave 1 inch clear along the length. Roll up steak and spinach jelly-roll fashion. Tie at 1-inch intervals with cotton kitchen string and cut crosswise into pieces about 2 inches wide.

● Clear a trench between the charcoal, and grill the pinwheels cut sides down over the clear space between the hot coals. Cook pinwheels 4 minutes on each cut side, brushing frequently with the marinade. Turn with tongs to brown the outsides, about 15 minutes in all. Add enough water to the remaining marinade to make a thin sauce, boil 5 minutes, and serve with the steaks.

PER SERVING: 439 CALORIES; 40 G PROTEIN; 8 G CARBOHYDRATES; 28 G TOTAL FAT; 9 G SATURATED FAT; 93 MG CHOLESTEROL; 1,036 MG SODIUM

Lamb Skewers with Lemons and Red Onions

MAKES 4 SERVINGS

This is a great recipe to prepare a day or two in advance of cooking. The lamb gets more tender and flavorful the longer it sits in the marinade.

1/4 cup extra virgin olive oil

2 large lemons, cut lengthwise into 6 wedges

12 bay leaves

3 large rosemary sprigs, cut into 1-inch lengths

1/2 teaspoon cracked black peppercorns

1/3 cup fresh lemon juice

1/3 cup water

kosher salt

1 1/4 pounds well trimmed boneless leg of lamb, cut into 1-inch cubes

1 small red onion, cut into 1-inch pieces

COOKS' TIPS:

- If your lamb is at room temperature, let the marinade cool before tossing in the cubes.

- You can substitute whole pearl onions for the red onions.

- Prepare a grill for barbecuing. In a medium saucepan, combine the olive oil with the lemon wedges, bay leaves, rosemary sprigs, and cracked peppercorns and heat to simmering. Pour into a shallow glass baking dish and stir in the lemon juice, water, and 1 teaspoon salt. Add the lamb and stir to coat. Cover with plastic wrap and marinate at least 15 minutes at room temperature or refrigerate 2 hours or overnight.

- Working over a foil-lined baking sheet, alternate the lamb on four 12-inch metal skewers with the lemon wedges, bay leaves, and pieces of red onion. Brush the kebabs with the lemon marinade. Grill over medium heat, turning once or twice and basting with marinade, until browned all over, 7 to 8 minutes for medium-rare meat. Serve immediately, but don't eat the bay leaves!

PER SERVING: 446 CALORIES; 21 G PROTEIN; 10 G CARBOHYDRATES; 38 G TOTAL FAT; 11 G SATURATED FAT; 81 MG CHOLESTEROL; 355 MG SODIUM

Feta-Lamb Kebabs with Yogurt Sauce

MAKES 6 SERVINGS

Packed with Eastern Mediterranean ingredients, these meatball kebabs are traditionally served inside pitas and drizzled with a spicy yogurt sauce. You can skip the bread, though, and pile them on plates of shredded lettuce.

1 1/2 *pounds ground lamb or beef*

1 *small onion, coarsely grated*

1 *large egg*

1 *cup peeled and finely chopped eggplant*

3/4 *cup crumbled feta cheese*

1/2 *cup seasoned bread crumbs*

2 *tablespoons chopped flat-leaf parsley*

1/2 *teaspoon salt*

1/2 *teaspoon freshly ground pepper*

pinch of cinnamon

oil for the grill

6 *large pitas, warmed and halved*

Classic Yogurt Sauce, recipe follows

• Prepare a grill for barbecuing. In a bowl, combine the meat, onion, egg, eggplant, cheese, bread crumbs, parsley, salt, pepper, and cinnamon. Mix gently but thoroughly with your hands and shape the mixture into 1 1/2-inch balls, wetting your hands if necessary to make shaping easier. Thread the meatballs onto 6 long, flat metal skewers or soak 12 shorter, thin wooden skewers in water 15 minutes and double-skewer the meatballs so they won't spin when you turn them.

• Oil the grill rack. Cook the kebabs over medium-high heat, turning occasionally, until cooked through, 10 to 15 minutes.

• Serve the meatballs in the pitas, with some Classic Yogurt Sauce on top.

LAMB AND PITAS ONLY, PER SERVING: 434 CALORIES; 25 G PROTEIN; 43 G CARBOHYDRATES; 17 G TOTAL FAT; 8 G SATURATED FAT; 107 MG CHOLESTEROL; 859 MG SODIUM

COOKS' TIP:

Grated onion adds a totally different flavor than even minced onion. Be sure to add all the onion juice to the meat mixture.

Classic Yogurt Sauce

MAKES 6 SERVINGS, ABOUT 1 CUP

You can make the sauce a day ahead. It's great with just about everything, from grilled lamb to roasted vegetables, and makes a good dip, too.

1 cup plain whole-milk yogurt, preferably Greek style
1/3 cup shredded mint or basil leaves
3/4 teaspoon ground cumin or coriander
1 garlic clove, crushed through a press
1 tablespoon fresh lemon juice, or more to taste
salt and freshly ground pepper to taste

● In a small bowl, mix the yogurt, mint, cumin, garlic, and lemon juice until blended. Season with salt and pepper. Taste and adjust lemon juice and seasoning if needed.

PER SERVING: 28 CALORIES; 2 G PROTEIN; 3 G CARBOHYDRATES; 1.5 G TOTAL FAT; 1 G SATURATED FAT; 5 MG CHOLESTEROL; 212 MG SODIUM

COOKS' TIP:

The garlic can overpower the sauce if it's a strong variety. Start with a small clove and taste the sauce. Add more if you like, but if you are making the sauce even just an hour ahead of serving, wait until serving to taste. You may not need more garlic.

Fruit and Nut Lamb Burgers

MAKES 4 SERVINGS

These are fun to make, beautiful to present, and delicious to eat. If you want to serve them on a bread, a Kaiser roll or pocketless pita will catch and hold the meat juices.

1 3/4 pounds ground lamb
2 tablespoons chopped dried cranberries
2 tablespoons chopped pistachios
2 tablespoons chopped Italian parsley
1 teaspoon finely grated orange zest
1 teaspoon salt
1/2 teaspoon ground cumin
1/2 teaspoon ground coriander
1/2 teaspoon lemon-pepper seasoning
vegetable oil

● Prepare a grill for barbecuing. Mix all ingredients, except the oil, together in a bowl until well combined. Pat into 4 thick patties. Place on a plate; cover with plastic wrap and refrigerate at least 15 minutes.

● Brush grill rack and burgers with oil. Grill burgers over medium-hot heat until inside registers 130° F on an instant-read thermometer, about 6 minutes on each side for medium-rare burgers.

PER SERVING: 446 CALORIES; 35 G PROTEIN; 2 G CARBOHYDRATES; 32 G TOTAL FAT; 12 G SATURATED FAT; 133 MG CHOLESTEROL; 730 MG SODIUM

Lamb Chops with Spicy Thai Peanut Sauce

MAKES 4 SERVINGS

If you can't find ginger marmalade, you can sweeten the sauce with honey and stir in some chopped candied ginger or grated fresh ginger.

1 tablespoon peanut oil plus extra for the grill

1 large shallot, finely chopped

1 large garlic clove, crushed through a press

1 cup chunky peanut butter

3 tablespoons ginger marmalade

1 tablespoon Asian chili-garlic sauce or Tabasco sauce

1 cup water

1/4 cup fresh lime juice

2 tablespoons soy sauce

8 loin lamb chops, 1-inch thick (about 4 ounces each)

COOKS' TIP:

The sauce is wonderful tossed with noodles—a pack of those quick-cooking ramen noodles are fine. Add some of the noodle cooking liquid (unseasoned) if the sauce gets too thick as the noodles soak it in.

- Prepare a grill for barbecuing. In a medium saucepan, heat the peanut oil until shimmering. Add the shallot and garlic and cook over medium heat, stirring, until golden, about 3 minutes. Remove from the heat and whisk in the peanut butter, marmalade, and chili-garlic sauce. Gradually whisk in the water. Simmer the sauce over medium-low heat until slightly thickened, about 10 minutes.

- Let the sauce cool slightly, then whisk in the lime juice and soy sauce.

- Place the lamb chops on a foil-lined baking sheet. Remove about 1/2 cup of the sauce to a small bowl and brush over the chops. Grill the chops over medium-high heat for 4 minutes per side, or until an instant-read thermometer inserted in the thickest part of a chop registers 130° F for medium rare. Transfer the chops to a platter. Spoon some warm peanut sauce over the lamb chops and serve, passing the extra sauce on the side.

PER SERVING: 685 CALORIES; 44 G PROTEIN; 26 G CARBOHYDRATES; 45 G TOTAL FAT; 10 G SATURATED FAT; 87 MG CHOLESTEROL; 921 MG SODIUM

Curried Honey-Mustard Lamb Loin

MAKES 4 SERVINGS

Once prohibitively expensive, whole lamb loins can be found at affordable prices in mega-stores or price-clubs such as BJ's and Costco. Ask friends who are members to check out their availability.

1 lamb loin, on the bone (about 2 pounds)
3 tablespoons vegetable oil plus extra for the grill
3 garlic cloves, minced
2 teaspoons curry powder
1¹/2 teaspoons kosher salt
2 tablespoons honey mustard
2 tablespoons torn fresh mint leaves

• Prepare a grill for barbecuing. Oil the grill rack. Place the lamb loin on a foil-lined baking sheet. In a small bowl, mix 2 tablespoons oil with the garlic. Add the curry powder and the kosher salt and mix well; rub the mixture over the meat. In another small bowl, mix the remaining 1 tablespoon oil with the honey mustard until blended and set aside.

• Grill the lamb loin over high heat 15 minutes, turning it every 5 minutes and searing the ends. Brush the meat side of the loin with the honey mustard mixture and grill 2 more minutes until the glaze is browned all over and an instant-read thermometer inserted in the center of the meat registers 140° F for medium-rare meat. Transfer the loin to a warm serving platter, and cover loosely with foil.

• Let the loin stand 10 minutes, then cut between the bones into chops. Sprinkle with the mint and serve.

PER SERVING: 313 CALORIES; 29 G PROTEIN; 6 G CARBOHYDRATES;
19 G TOTAL FAT; 4 G SATURATED FAT; 90 MG CHOLESTEROL; 1,004 MG SODIUM

Spiced Lamb Chops

MAKES 4 SERVINGS

The spice mix called *ras al hanout* translates as "head of the shop" because traditionally the proprietors of Moroccan spice shops made their own unique seasoning blends. You can be your own mix-master and use your favorite herbs and spices if you can't find prepared ras al hanout or the time to make your own.

2 tablespoons vegetable oil

8 thick lamb loin chops (2 pounds total)

2 teaspoons ras al hanout (Moroccan spice mix, recipe page 204)

1 1/4 teaspoons kosher salt

3 garlic cloves, minced

1 tablespoon chopped cilantro

● Prepare a grill for barbecuing. Oil the grill rack. Place the lamb chops on a foil-lined baking sheet and brush on both sides with remaining oil. Season generously on both sides with the spice mix, salt, minced garlic, and cilantro.

● Grill the lamb chops over high heat, turning them once, until browned all over, about 7 minutes in all for medium-rare meat. Transfer the lamb chops to a warm serving platter to serve.

PER SERVING: 332 CALORIES; 41 G PROTEIN; 1 G CARBOHYDRATES; 17 G TOTAL FAT; 5 G SATURATED FAT; 129 MG CHOLESTEROL; 838 MG SODIUM

COOKS' TIP:

You can season 1 pound of ground lamb, which can be made into 4 patties or 16 small meatballs, with the spice mix and grill them the same way as the chops. If you skewer the meatballs, you should cook them about 4 minutes, turning them every minute.

PREP TIME: 35 MINUTES   COOKING TIME: 8 MINUTES

Lamb Teriyaki with Mushrooms

MAKES 6 SERVINGS

You can use bottled teriyaki sauce or roasted-garlic teriyaki sauce if you're short on time.

1/4 *cup low-sodium soy sauce*

1/4 *cup rice wine vinegar*

1 *tablespoon grated peeled fresh gingerroot*

1 *small garlic clove, crushed through a press*

1 1/2 *pounds lean leg of lamb, cut into* 3/4-*inch cubes*

2 *tablespoons vegetable oil*

12 *ounces cleaned cremini or other white mushrooms,*
   stems trimmed even with the cap

8 *red cherry tomatoes*

1 *yellow bell pepper, cut into* 3/4-*inch squares*

8 *scallions, trimmed, cut into 1-inch pieces*

● Prepare a grill for barbecuing. Soak bamboo or wooden skewers in water for 15 minutes. Mix soy sauce, vinegar, gingerroot, and garlic in a bowl. Add lamb and toss to coat. Marinate for 15 minutes at room temperature or covered with plastic wrap 2 hours or longer in refrigerator.

● Grease the grill rack with oil. Thread lamb onto skewers, reserving marinade and alternating pieces with mushrooms, tomatoes, bell pepper, and scallions. Brush with oil. Grill 4 inches from heat 3 to 4 minutes per side, basting occasionally with marinade.

PER SERVING: 349 CALORIES; 26 G PROTEIN; 8 G CARBOHYDRATES; 24 G TOTAL FAT; 8 G SATURATED FAT; 91 MG CHOLESTEROL; 332 MG SODIUM

COOKS' TIP:

Add more scallions if you like. They go well with every bite of lamb and mushroom.

PREP TIME: 20 MINUTES   COOKING TIME: 22 MINUTES

Mustard-Crusted Lamb Rack

MAKES 4 SERVINGS

You will have to drop everything and focus on the meat as it cooks. You can, however, grill some vegetables while you are grilling the lamb and just pull the vegetables to a cool spot on the grill in the moments you tend to the lamb.

1/4 cup extra virgin olive oil plus extra for the grill
1 rack of lamb (1 1/2 pounds, 8 ribs), ends of bones
*   scraped clean*
2 tablespoons finely minced rosemary
salt and freshly cracked black pepper
1/3 cup whole grain Dijon mustard
2 tablespoons chopped parsley
2 tablespoons snipped chives
2 tablespoons shredded fresh mint

COOKS' TIP:

Make sure the meat is at room temperature so it will cook evenly.

• Prepare a grill for barbecuing with coals in two sections, hot and medium. Or prepare to move the coals to one side after the initial searing. Oil the grill rack.

• Place the lamb on a foil-lined baking sheet. Mix 1/4 cup oil, the rosemary, and a generous amount of salt and pepper in a small bowl and rub or brush all over the lamb. Wrap the ends of the bones with foil so they won't burn.

• Hold the lamb with one end down on the grill over high heat to sear the meat. Repeat with the other end. Place fat side down and grill over high heat until the fat is crisp and browned, about 5 minutes. Turn the lamb, cover the grill, and cook over medium heat 10 minutes. Slather the mustard over the fat side of the lamb. Cook mustard side down, covered, 5 minutes, until the inside registers 130° F on an instant-read thermometer for medium rare. Remove rack to a cutting board, cover loosely with foil, and let stand 5 minutes. Mix the parsley, chives, and mint and sprinkle over the mustard side. Slice between every 2 of the bones to serve double chops.

PER SERVING: 450 CALORIES; 20 G PROTEIN; 2 G CARBOHYDRATES;
40 G TOTAL FAT; 12 G SATURATED FAT; 85 MG CHOLESTEROL; 298 MG SODIUM

PREP TIME: 25 MINUTES   COOKING TIME: 12 MINUTES

Lamb Chops with Fennel and Parmigiano Reggiano Butter

MAKES 4 SERVINGS

Thick lamb chops are ideal for grilling because they are easy to heat through without overcooking. Turn them every minute once they have browned well on each side, and don't forget to turn them so they will cook on their fat side, even though you may have to recruit a helper or two to steady them with tongs as the fat renders and browns.

8 well trimmed lamb chops, about 1 1/2 inches thick
* (4 ounces each)*
2 to 3 tablespoons lemon-pepper seasoning
extra virgin olive oil
Fennel and Parmigiano Reggiano Butter,
* recipe follows*

● Prepare a grill for barbecuing. Place the chops on a foil-lined baking sheet and generously sprinkle lemon-pepper seasoning on both sides. Press the seasoning into the meat and set aside for 10 to 15 minutes.

● Oil a grill rack and brush chops on both sides with oil. Grill over medium-high heat, turning as the first side gets crusty and browned, about 6 minutes. Cook on the second side 6 minutes for medium rare. Transfer to a warm platter and cover loosely with foil. Let stand 5 minutes. Serve with Fennel and Parmigiano Reggiano Butter.

PER SERVING: 400 CALORIES; 47 G PROTEIN; 0 G CARBOHYDRATES;
22 G TOTAL FAT; 8 G SATURATED FAT; 155 MG CHOLESTEROL; 599 MG SODIUM

Fennel and Parmigiano Reggiano Butter

MAKES 4 SERVINGS

You can make the butter a day ahead of serving. Let it soften at room temperature so it will melt quickly on the hot lamb. Whisk it again before serving so it looks silky.

1 stick (4 ounces) unsalted butter, softened

1 tablespoon fresh lemon juice

1/2 cup diced fresh fennel

1/3 cup freshly grated Parmigiano Reggiano cheese

2 tablespoons snipped fennel fern

salt and freshly ground pepper to taste

● In a medium bowl, whisk the butter with the lemon juice until blended. Fold in the fennel, cheese, and fennel fern. Season with salt and pepper.

PER SERVING: 249 CALORIES; 4 G PROTEIN; 2 G CARBOHYDRATES; 26 G TOTAL FAT; 6 G SATURATED FAT; 69 MG CHOLESTEROL; 313 MG SODIUM

COOKS' TIP:

Reserve enough large fennel ferns (wrap them in a paper towel after rinsing and store in the crisper) to garnish the dish you serve with the butter.

Provençal Burgers

MAKES 4 SERVINGS

Although each region and cook in Provence, in southwest France, has its own formula for the area's flavorful and fragrant herb mixture, a "basic" herbes de Provence contains 1 bay leaf; 1 tablespoon each dried rosemary, basil, marjoram, summer savory, and oregano; 2 teaspoons dried thyme leaves; and 1/2 teaspoon each fennel seeds, lavender, ground coriander, and freshly ground white pepper. You can make up a large batch and give it as gifts and you and your friends will save beaucoup bucks.

3/4 pound ground pork

1/4 pound ground lamb

2 large shallots, minced

2 tablespoons dry red wine

1 tablespoon minced flat-leaf parsley

1 teaspoon lemon-pepper seasoning

1 teaspoon finely chopped herbes de Provence
  (store-bought or homemade)

● Prepare a grill for barbecuing. In a large bowl, gently mix the pork and lamb with the remaining ingredients. Shape the mixture into 4 patties.

● Grill burgers until cooked through, about 10 minutes, turning once.

PER SERVING: 275 CALORIES; 23 G PROTEIN; 2 G CARBOHYDRATES; 18 G TOTAL FAT; 7 G SATURATED FAT; 85 MG CHOLESTEROL; 149 MG SODIUM

PREP TIME: 10 MINUTES   COOKING TIME: 15 MINUTES

Pork Tenderloins with Syrah-Date Sauce

MAKES 4 SERVINGS

Pork tenderloin is a griller's best friend. It is basically waste-free and guaranteed to be tender. Since the small end cooks more quickly than the large one, place it over cooler coals or fold it under and tie it with kitchen string.

2 tablespoons extra virgin olive oil plus extra for the grill

2 pork tenderloins (³/4 pound each), silverskin removed

2 teaspoons Spanish smoked paprika or hot or sweet Hungarian paprika

fine sea salt and freshly ground pepper

SYRAH-DATE SAUCE

8 pitted Medjool dates

2 tablespoons coarsely chopped smoked almonds

1 cup Syrah or other dry red wine

1 cinnamon stick

● Prepare a grill for barbecuing. Oil the grill rack. Rub the tenderloins with the oil and then the paprika, salt, and pepper. Grill over medium heat, turning every 5 minutes, until cooked through, about 15 minutes. Remove from the grill and place on a cutting board. Cover loosely with foil and let stand 10 minutes before slicing.

● While pork cooks, make the Syrah-Date Sauce: Stuff the dates with the almonds and place in a small saucepan. Add the wine and cinnamon stick and simmer over medium heat until reduced to ¹/3 cup, about 10 minutes. Serve the pork with the sauce and dates.

TENDERLOIN ONLY, PER SERVING: 219 CALORIES; 24 G PROTEIN;
3 G CARBOHYDRATES; 13 G TOTAL FAT; 2 G SATURATED FAT;
66 MG CHOLESTEROL; 832 MG SODIUM
SYRAH-DATE SAUCE, PER SERVING: 182 CALORIES; 2 G PROTEIN;
34 G CARBOHYDRATES; 2 G TOTAL FAT; 0 G SATURATED FAT;
0 MG CHOLESTEROL; 4 MG SODIUM

COOKS' TIP:

If you can't find the luscious Medjool dates, you can use chopped dates or the whole, pitted Deglet Noor variety. Their skins are papery and you will have to tear them off for a better presentation.

Chili-Brine Pork Chops with Tasty Fresh Salsa

MAKES 4 SERVINGS

A kitchen syringe costs only a few dollars and it's the only tool to use to inject the brine into the pork. If you leave the pork for 4 to 6 hours in the refrigerator, the brine will penetrate the muscles, and by osmosis, flavor and tenderize the meat. The retained water will also keep the chops moist when cooked. Tests prove that even if the pork is cooked immediately after injecting, it will be noticeably moister, more flavorful and tender than pork treated with a dry rub and brushed with oil.

CHILE BRINE

1 tablespoon ancho chile powder
1 teaspoon salt
1/4 teaspoon ground cumin
1/8 teaspoon freshly ground pepper
pinch of allspice
pinch of cinnamon
1/4 cup boiling water

4 rib pork chops, 1 inch thick
*1 tablespoon extra virgin olive oil plus extra for
  the grill*

TASTY FRESH SALSA

*6 large ripe plum tomatoes, seeded and coarsely
  chopped*
3 jalapeños, seeded and finely chopped
finely grated zest and juice of 1 lime
1/2 large white onion, finely chopped
3 tablespoons finely chopped cilantro
2 garlic cloves, crushed through a press
1/2 teaspoon dried oregano
salt and freshly ground pepper

• Prepare a grill for barbecuing. In a small bowl, prepare the Chile Brine: Mix the chili powder, salt, cumin, pepper, allspice, and cinnamon and add the boiling water. Stir until the salt dissolves. Place the brine into a kitchen syringe.

• Inject about 1 tablespoon of the brine into the center of each chop through the side. Rub the outside of the chops with the oil. If you don't have a kitchen syringe, omit the water and rub the oil and then the spice mixture all over the pork chops.

• Oil the grill rack. Grill the chops 4 minutes on each side over medium-high heat.

• While chops cook, in a medium bowl, prepare the Tasty Fresh Salsa by mixing all the ingredients. Serve with the chops.

CHOPS ALONE, PER SERVING: 343 CALORIES; 42 G PROTEIN;
1 G CARBOHYDRATES; 18 G TOTAL FAT; 5 G SATURATED FAT;
115 MG CHOLESTEROL; 689 MG SODIUM
SALSA, PER SERVING: 34 CALORIES; 1 G PROTEIN; 8 G CARBOHYDRATES;
0 G TOTAL FAT; 0 G SATURATED FAT; 0 MG CHOLESTEROL; 300 MG SODIUM

COOKS' TIP:

The chile brine and salsa combo is one of millions of flavor and condiment possibilities. Check out the other brine recipes in this book and purchase or make your own chutneys, relishes, salsas, and sauces to complement the grilled chops.

PREP TIME: 10 MINUTES   COOKING TIME: 8 MINUTES

Taco'd Pork Kebabs

MAKES 6 SERVINGS

Unthread the kebabs right into a flour tortilla if you want. Hold the tortilla in one hand and use it to grab and pull off the line of ingredients.

vegetable oil for the grill
1 envelope taco seasoning mix
1/4 cup olive oil plus additional for brushing
2 pork tenderloins (1 pound each), silverskin removed and cut into 1-inch cubes
1 red bell pepper, seeded, cut into 1-inch squares
1 yellow bell pepper, seeded, cut into 1-inch squares
6 fat scallions, trimmed and cut into 1 1/2-inch pieces
2 limes, each cut into 6 wedges

• Prepare a grill for barbecue. Grease the rack with oil.

• Blend the taco seasoning mix with the olive oil in a large bowl, add the pork, and toss to coat. Thread meat, bell peppers, scallions, and lime wedges onto 6 skewers, 12 inches in length. Brush the kebabs with olive oil and grill over a hot fire, turning occasionally, until lightly charred and cooked through, about 8 minutes.

PER SERVING: 273 CALORIES; 25 G PROTEIN; 12 G CARBOHYDRATES;
15 G TOTAL FAT; 2 G SATURATED FAT; 66 MG CHOLESTEROL; 565 MG SODIUM

Pork with Green Curry Sauce and Grilled Mango

MAKES 4 SERVINGS WITH ABOUT 2 CUPS SAUCE

Bottled curry sauces help get the jump on many delicious dinners. Stir a spoonful of sauce into mayonnaise for your next chicken or shrimp salad or use some to make a dip for fruit by flavoring sour cream or crème fraîche.

grapeseed oil
2 pork tenderloins (1 pound each), silverskin removed
salt and freshly ground pepper
1 cup canned coconut milk
2 1/2 tablespoons bottled green curry paste
1/2 cup fresh cilantro leaves
1/2 cup chicken stock or low-sodium broth
2 unpeeled mangos, pits removed
3 tablespoons sweetened condensed milk
1 red jalapeño, seeded and minced
peel from 1 lime, slivered
4 tablespoons fresh lime juice

• Prepare a grill for barbecuing. Oil the grill rack. To butterfly the pork, place tenderloins on a cutting board and cut a little over halfway through lengthwise. Open up and flatten gently with a meat mallet; the meat should be about 1/2-inch thick. Place the pork on a foil-lined baking sheet and sprinkle with salt and pepper.

• Place the coconut milk, green curry paste, and cilantro in a blender and blend until smooth. Remove 1/4 cup of the mixture to a cup and add 1 tablespoon grapeseed oil. Brush the mixture over both sides of the tenderloins. Grill the pork over high heat on both sides until browned and cooked through, about 5 minutes in all. Remove to a platter, cover loosely with foil, and let stand 5 minutes.

• Place remaining coconut-milk mixture in a small saucepan, whisk in the stock and heat to boiling. Keep warm while the fruit cooks.

• Score the cut sides of the mangos with a knife to make crosshatched cuts to the skin but not through it. Mix the condensed milk, jalapeño, half the lime peel, and half the lime juice in a cup. Lightly brush the cut side of the fruit with grapeseed oil and place cut side down over hot heat. Cook 1 minute, turn over and cook until heated through, about 45 seconds. While fruit is heating, brush the cut sides with the jalapeño mixture and grill until caramelized, about 30 seconds. Remove from the heat and set aside.

• To serve: Slice the pork and place on a platter. Press on the skin side of the mango halves to pop the fruit out in a curve so you can cut off the cubes. Place in a bowl and sprinkle with the remaining slivered lime peel and lime juice. Serve the mango and the sauce with the pork.

PER SERVING: 487 CALORIES; 40 G PROTEIN; 35 G CARBOHYDRATES; 23 G TOTAL FAT; 15 G SATURATED FAT; 104 MG CHOLESTEROL; 1,046 MG SODIUM

PREP TIME: 30 MINUTES   COOKING TIME: 10 MINUTES

Grilled-Arugula and Prosciutto Calzones

MAKES 4 SERVINGS

A calzone is a half-moon shaped stuffed pizza that originated in Naples. The filling can be just about anything, from sausage and thick tomato sauce to all cheese. Here, spicy arugula (you can use watercress or young dandelion leaves instead) is grilled to intensify its flavor and soften its texture.

2 tablespoons extra virgin olive oil plus extra
    for brushing
1 pound frozen pizza dough, thawed, cut into
    4 pieces (recipe, page 171)
1/2 pound fresh ricotta cheese, drained
1/4 pound whole-milk mozzarella cheese, shredded
1/4 cup freshly grated Parmigiano Reggiano cheese
2 ounces thinly sliced prosciutto di Parma or other
    ham, coarsely chopped
1 bunch arugula, rinsed, tough ends trimmed
salt and freshly ground pepper
garlic salt for sprinkling
vegetable oil for brushing the grill

● Prepare a grill for barbecuing. Place a vegetable grilling pan on the grill to preheat. Brush two baking sheets with olive oil. On a lightly floured work surface, roll out one piece of dough to an 8-inch round about 1/4-inch thick and place on a prepared baking sheet. Repeat with remaining dough.

● In a small bowl, mix the ricotta, mozzarella, Parmigiano Reggiano, and prosciutto. Place the arugula on a foil-lined baking sheet and drizzle with 2 tablespoons olive oil. Sprinkle with salt and pepper and toss to mix. Place the arugula in the hot grill pan and grill over hot coals, turning with tongs, until wilted, about 3 minutes. Return to the foil-lined baking sheet, and then place on a cutting board. Coarsely chop the arugula and stir it into the ricotta mixture.

● Brush the dough rounds on both sides with olive oil. Place the dough rounds and filling near the grill. Grill 2 dough rounds at a time 2 to 3 minutes on one side, until lightly charred and barely crisp. Turn rounds over and slide onto a baking sheet. Repeat with remaining dough rounds.

● Divide filling over rounds and fold over to form half-moon calzones. Press edges together, brush on both sides with olive oil, and sprinkle lightly with garlic salt. Brush the grill with vegetable oil. Grill over low heat, turning frequently, until cheese is melted and dough is cooked, 3 to 4 minutes in all. Place on a platter or wooden cutting board and serve.

PER SERVING: 471 CALORIES; 23 G PROTEIN; 40 G CARBOHYDRATES;
25 G TOTAL FAT; 11 G SATURATED FAT; 64 MG CHOLESTEROL; 759 MG SODIUM

PREP TIME: 10 MINUTES   COOKING TIME: 8 MINUTES

Seared Pork and Pickled Pepper Panini

MAKES 6 SANDWICHES

Panino is the Italian word for small bread, and *panini* is the plural. Instead of toasting them in a sandwich press, these little sandwiches are cooked on a grill and contain a grilled filling for good measure.

2 pork tenderloins (3/4 pound each), sliced on the
    diagonal 3/4-inch thick, slices pounded to 1/4-inch
    thickness
1/4 cup extra virgin olive oil plus extra for the grill
kosher salt and freshly ground pepper
1 stick (4 ounces) unsalted butter, softened
12 slices of Italian country bread (1/4-inch thick),
    cut from 1 oval loaf
1/2 cup sliced stemmed pickled red and green peppers
12 slices queso blanco or Provolone cheese

● Prepare a grill for barbecuing. Place the pork on a foil-lined baking sheet, brush on both sides with oil and season with salt and pepper. Brush the grill rack with oil and grill the pork over high heat until browned and no longer pink in the center, about 1 minute per side. Transfer to a plate.

● Spread 2 teaspoons of butter on one side of each slice of bread. Lay 6 slices on a work surface, buttered side down. Top each of the slices with one-sixth of the pork and pickled pepper and 2 slices of cheese. Close the sandwiches with the remaining bread slices, buttered side up.

● In batches, place sandwiches on the grill to one side of medium coals and set a heavy cast-iron griddle or skillet directly on top of the sandwiches to weigh them down. Cook the panini for 3 minutes. Flip each sandwich and cook for about 3 minutes longer, or until browned and crisp all over. (The cheese should be hot but not melted.) Transfer the panini to a cutting board and cut them in half. Repeat with the remaining panini, reducing the heat to moderate.

PER SERVING: 705 CALORIES; 40 G PROTEIN; 34 G CARBOHYDRATES; 46 G TOTAL
FAT; 22 G SATURATED FAT; 1,423 MG CHOLESTEROL; 1,157 MG SODIUM

Pork Chops with Pomegranate Glaze

MAKES 4 SERVINGS

Pomegranate juice is available in the produce section of even small grocery stores so you don't have to cut and squeeze the fresh fruit. Pomegranate molasses is available in Middle Eastern grocery stores. If you can't find it, boil 1 cup pomegranate juice with 1 tablespoon sugar until it is thick.

2 tablespoons vegetable oil plus extra for the grill

1 medium onion, minced

2 large garlic cloves, minced

1 1/2 cups pomegranate juice, or ruby port, or
*   cranberry-raspberry juice*

2 tablespoons pomegranate molasses or maple syrup

1/4 teaspoon ground allspice

salt and freshly ground pepper

1 tablespoon fresh lemon juice

8 boneless pork chops, 1/2 inch thick

pomegranate seeds for garnish

chopped pistachios for garnish

COOKS' TIP:

You can use any juice and a syrupy version of it such as orange juice and orange liqueur, lemon juice and limoncello, or lime juice and bottled sweetened lime juice.

- Prepare a grill for barbecue. Grease the rack with oil.

- Prepare the pomegranate glaze: In a small saucepan, heat 1 tablespoon of the oil until shimmering. Add the onion and garlic and cook over medium-high heat until golden, about 5 minutes. Add 1 cup of the pomegranate juice, the molasses, and the allspice; simmer 5 minutes. Pour 1/2 cup of the mixture into a glass measuring cup; stir in the remaining 1 tablespoon oil. Set aside. Add the remaining 1/2 cup pomegranate juice, the salt, pepper, and lemon juice to the mixture in the saucepan and keep the sauce gently simmering.

- Place the pork chops on a foil-lined baking sheet and brush with reserved pomegranate mixture. Grill chops over medium-high heat, turning and basting with the glaze until cooked through and glaze is caramelized, about 7 minutes (be careful not to overcook). Remove to a platter, cover loosely with foil, and let stand 5 minutes. Sprinkle with the pomegranate seeds and pistachios. Serve with the warm pomegranate sauce.

PER SERVING: 455 CALORIES; 45 G PROTEIN; 35 G CARBOHYDRATES; 25 G TOTAL FAT; 6 G SATURATED FAT; 115 MG CHOLESTEROL; 405 MG SODIUM

PREP TIME: 10 MINUTES   COOKING TIME: 12 MINUTES

Pork Medallions with Orange-Chile Sauce

MAKES 4 SERVINGS

Sweet pork is divine simply seasoned, but it can meet and match even the most brazen of flavors. A triple-dose of orange helps to temper the fiery chiles in the sauce for the grilled meat.

1 tablespoon grated orange zest

1/4 cup fresh orange juice

2 tablespoons grapeseed, or canola or peanut oil,
*   plus extra for the grill*

1 tablespoon sambal oelek or other Asian-style
*   chile sauce*

4 boneless pork loin chops, 1 1/4-inch thick
*   (2 pounds total)*

kosher salt and freshly ground pepper

1 navel orange, thinly sliced crosswise

● Prepare a grill for barbecuing. In a small bowl, mix the orange zest, orange juice, 2 tablespoons oil, and the sambal oelek. Place the chops on a foil-lined baking sheet, sprinkle with salt and pepper, and brush on both sides with the orange mixture. Grill the chops over medium-high heat for 6 minutes per side, until browned and cooked through, turning every 2 minutes and brushing with remaining orange mixture before turning. Transfer to a warm platter, garnish with the orange slices, and serve.

PER SERVING: 313 CALORIES; 29 G PROTEIN; 6 G CARBOHYDRATES; 19 G TOTAL FAT; 4 G SATURATED FAT; 90 MG CHOLESTEROL; 1,004 MG SODIUM

COOKS' TIP:

Try the sauce as a dip for grilled shrimp, bell pepper strips, or pineapple.

Grilled-Portobello and Pancetta Soup

MAKES 6 SERVINGS

Pancetta is an Italian unsmoked bacon that is salted and spiced. If you can't find it, you can use bacon, preferably applewood smoked, or slices of baked ham.

24 medium porcini or cremini mushrooms

3 tablespoons extra virgin olive oil

3 garlic cloves, crushed through a press

salt and freshly ground pepper

1 medium carrot, peeled, cut into 1/8-inch rounds

1 celery rib, cut crosswise into 1-inch pieces

1 red onion, sliced 1/4-inch thick

1 thyme sprig

4 cups chicken stock or broth

vegetable oil for grill

3 ounces thinly sliced pancetta

1/4 cup heavy cream

• Prepare a grill for barbecuing. Place 2 vegetable grill pans on the grill to preheat. Place mushrooms on a foil-lined baking sheet. Mix olive oil, the garlic, and salt and pepper in a cup and drizzle 2 tablespoons of the mixture over the mushrooms. Toss to coat. Spread out the mushrooms in a grill pan and cook over medium-high heat, stirring once, until charred and tender, about 15 minutes.

• While mushrooms cook, place carrot, celery, and onion slices on the foil-lined baking sheet and toss with remaining olive oil mixture. Grill the vegetables in the second grill pan until charred and tender, about 15 minutes, stirring occasionally.

• Place the mushrooms and vegetables in a 3-quart saucepan, add the thyme and stock, and bring to a boil. Cover the pan partially and simmer over low heat for 10 minutes. Discard the thyme.

• While the soup simmers, brush the grill with vegetable oil and grill the pancetta until crisp. Place on a cutting board and cut into short shreds. Add the heavy cream to the soup. Working in batches, purée the soup in a blender. Return the soup to the saucepan and bring to a gentle simmer. Season with salt and pepper and serve hot, garnished with the pancetta.

PER SERVING: 220 CALORIES; 14 G PROTEIN; 15 G CARBOHYDRATES; 13 G TOTAL FAT; 3 G SATURATED FAT; 9 MG CHOLESTEROL; 836 MG SODIUM

Vegetables

Green Beans with Onions and Pancetta

MAKES 4 SERVINGS

It is amazing how grilling concentrates the flavor of vegetables, elevating even the basic green bean to "ooh" and "ah" status. You will want to purchase a vegetable grill pan just for green-bean duty!

1/4 cup extra virgin olive oil plus extra for the grill

1 1/2 pounds green beans, trimmed

1 large red onion, cut crosswise into 1/2-inch thick slices, rings separated

1/4 pound thinly sliced pancetta

1 teaspoon dried oregano

salt and freshly ground pepper

4 large roasted garlic cloves (recipe, page 165)

1/4 teaspoon crushed red pepper

- Prepare a grill for barbecuing. Oil the grill rack and a vegetable grilling pan and preheat the pan on the grill.

- Heat 2 quarts salted water to boiling in a saucepan and cook the green beans and onions 5 minutes.

- While vegetables parboil, spread out the pancetta on a foil-lined baking sheet and brush on both sides with some of the oil. Grill until browned and crisp over hot heat about 30 seconds on each side. Remove to a cutting board, cut crosswise into 1/2-inch strips and set aside.

- Drain the vegetables in a colander and rinse with cold water. Pat dry and place in a bowl. Drizzle with 1 tablespoon of the oil and sprinkle with the oregano, salt, and pepper. Toss to coat and spread out in the hot grill pan. Cook over hot heat until vegetables are tender, tossing frequently, about 10 minutes.

- Mix the remaining oil with the garlic, red pepper, salt, and pepper, mashing the garlic with a fork until the dressing is smooth. Add the vegetables and pancetta and toss to mix.

PER SERVING: 249 CALORIES; 7 G PROTEIN; 16 G CARBOHYDRATES; 19 G TOTAL FAT; 3 G SATURATED FAT; 8 MG CHOLESTEROL; 452 MG SODIUM

COOKS' TIP:

You can freeze the Italian unsmoked bacon called pancetta so you will have it on hand. To thaw only what you need and thaw it quickly, spread out two slices between two sheets of parchment and stack up the remaining pieces in similar fashion. Wrap the stack in foil and place in a zip-top freezer bag. Freeze up to six months, removing only what you need when you need it.

PREP TIME: 10 MINUTES   COOKING TIME: 4 MINUTES

Squash Ribbons with Tapenade

MAKES 4 SERVINGS

Be sure to arrange the squash pieces perpendicular to the grill grid so they won't fall into the fire.

1/2 *pound medium summer squash or yellow zucchini, thinly sliced lengthwise*

1/2 *pound medium zucchini, thinly sliced lengthwise*

1/4 *cup plus 2 tablespoons extra virgin olive oil plus extra for the grill*

1/4 *cup bottled tapenade (Provençal olive and anchovy spread)*

1/4 *cup finely diced red bell pepper*

2 *tablespoons coarsely chopped parsley*

coarse sea salt

freshly grated Parmigiano Reggiano cheese

lemon wedges for serving

• Prepare a grill for barbecuing. Place the squash and zucchini slices on a foil-lined baking sheet and brush on both sides with 1/4 cup oil.

• In a large bowl, mix the tapenade, bell pepper, parsley, and 2 tablespoons of the oil. Set aside.

• Oil the grill rack and grill the squash and zucchini slices over hot heat until tender and browned, about 4 minutes, turning every minute. Remove to bowl with tapenade and toss to coat. Season with salt and sprinkle with cheese. Serve with lemon wedges.

PER SERVING: 95 CALORIES; 7 G PROTEIN; 9 G CARBOHYDRATES; 5 G TOTAL FAT; 3 G SATURATED FAT; 10 MG CHOLESTEROL; 600 MG SODIUM

Garlic-Grilled Bell Peppers

MAKES 4 SERVINGS

Freeze some fresh summer peppers to enjoy this dish year-round. Pack them in freezer bags without the dressing in family-size amounts.

2 large green bell peppers

2 large yellow bell peppers

2 large red bell peppers

1/3 cup extra virgin olive oil

1/4 cup tightly packed basil leaves, torn into small pieces

2 garlic cloves, crushed through a press

salt and freshly ground pepper

● Prepare grill for barbecuing. Grill peppers over hot heat as close to the coals as possible, turning the peppers frequently with tongs, until blackened and blistered on all sides, about 15 minutes.

● Transfer the peppers to a strainer set over a medium bowl, cover with plastic wrap and let the peppers steam for 10 minutes.

● Remove the peppers to a plate. Working over the strainer to collect the juices, peel the peppers and discard the stems and seeds.

● Cut the peppers lengthwise into 1/2-inch-wide strips and add to the bowl with the juices. Add the olive oil, basil, and garlic. Season the peppers generously with salt and pepper and toss gently to mix.

PER SERVING: 217 CALORIES; 2 G PROTEIN; 12 G CARBOHYDRATES; 19 G TOTAL FAT; 1 G SATURATED FAT; 0 MG CHOLESTEROL; 582 MG SODIUM

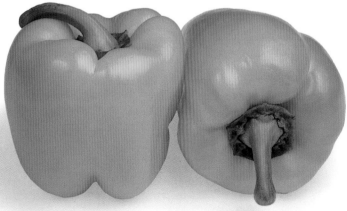

Roasted Potato Wedges

MAKES 6 SERVINGS

It takes more time than most people have to stand by the grill and cook raw potatoes until tender, but not burned. Here's a recipe for efficient cooks: Blanched potatoes crisp up quickly and get plenty of flavor, plus glamorous grill marks over the coals.

2 tablespoons olive oil plus extra for the grill
2 pounds medium Yukon Gold potatoes, each cut
  lengthwise into 6 wedges
kosher salt and freshly ground black pepper
1/2 teaspoon cayenne pepper
1 cup freshly grated imported Asiago or
  Provolone cheese
1/4 cup snipped fresh chives

- Prepare a grill for barbecuing. Oil the grill rack and a vegetable grilling pan and preheat the pan on the grill.

- Heat 2 quarts salted water to boiling in a saucepan and cook the potatoes until almost tender when pierced with a toothpick, about 5 minutes. Drain and place in a large bowl. Drizzle with oil, sprinkle with salt, pepper, and cayenne, and toss gently to coat. Spread out in the preheated grill pan and grill over medium heat until charred and tender, about 15 minutes.

- Transfer potatoes to a bowl and drizzle with oil. Toss to coat. Sprinkle the potatoes with the cheese and chives. Toss gently to mix.

PER SERVING: 238 CALORIES; 9 G PROTEIN; 28 G CARBOHYDRATES; 11 G TOTAL FAT; 4 G SATURATED FAT; 15 MG CHOLESTEROL; 202 MG SODIUM

Grilled Plantain Tostones

MAKES 6 SERVINGS

Traditionally fried two times, tostones are a favorite side dish on Hispanic tables from Cuba to Puerto Rico. Here the plantains get their first cooking by boiling and their second, after the boiled pieces are gently crushed, on the grill. You can also grill them uncrushed, if you'd like.

12 diagonal slices green plantain, 1 inch thick
1/3 cup extra virgin olive oil
2 tablespoons fresh lemon juice
1/2 teaspoon chili powder
2 garlic cloves, crushed through a press or
   1/2 teaspoon granulated garlic
salt and freshly ground pepper

● Prepare a grill for barbecuing. In a large saucepan of boiling salted water, cook the plantains until just tender, when a thin skewer pierces them easily, about 8 minutes. Drain and let cool. Using the heel of your hand, flatten each plantain slice to about 1/2 inch. Place on a foil-lined baking sheet.

● In a small bowl, whisk the olive oil with the lemon juice, chili powder, and garlic and season with salt and pepper. Brush the plantains generously with the dressing.

● Grill the plantains over a medium-hot fire until crisp and caramelized, about 3 minutes per side. Sprinkle with salt and serve at once.

PER SERVING: 186 CALORIES; 1 G PROTEIN; 20 G CARBOHYDRATES; 13 G TOTAL FAT; 1 G SATURATED FAT; 0 MG CHOLESTEROL; 197 MG SODIUM

PREP TIME: 10 MINUTES   COOKING TIME: 4 MINUTES

Grilled Asparagus with Eggs Mimosa

MAKES 4 SERVINGS

The classic egg-yolk garnish is named because it resembles the yellow flower of the mimosa tree. It's a pity to leave the whites out of the picture, so they are sieved separately onto the asparagus.

oil for the grill
1¹/2 pounds pencil-thin asparagus (see Cooks' Tip)
3 tablespoons bottled citrus vinaigrette dressing
sea salt and freshly ground pepper
2 hard-cooked eggs, shelled, whites and yolks
  separated
smoked Spanish paprika or other hot or sweet
  paprika for sprinkling
lemon wedges for serving

● Prepare a grill for barbecue. Oil the grill rack and a vegetable grilling pan; set the pan on the grill to heat.

● Spread out the asparagus on a foil-lined baking sheet and drizzle with the dressing. Season with salt and pepper. Spread out the asparagus in the hot grill pan and grill over high heat for 4 minutes, or until just tender.

● Arrange asparagus on a platter. Place the egg whites in a fine metal sieve and hold the sieve over the asparagus. Press the whites through, moving the sieve so the whites fall evenly over the asparagus. Repeat with the yolks. Sprinkle with the paprika, salt, and pepper. Serve with lemon wedges.

PER SERVING: 134 CALORIES; 8 G PROTEIN; 12 G CARBOHYDRATES;
8 G TOTAL FAT; 2 G SATURATED FAT; 106 MG CHOLESTEROL; 411 MG SODIUM

COOKS' TIP:

To cook thicker asparagus spears, add 1 to 2 minutes to the grilling time.

Grilled Radicchio with Gorgonzola and Walnuts

MAKES 4 SERVINGS

Radicchio gets a total makeover when it is grilled. The leaves wilt and char to make an even more dramatic appearance and the natural bitterness turns into juicy sweetness.

1/4 cup extra virgin olive oil plus extra for the grill
    and drizzling
2 large heads of radicchio (about 3/4 pound each),
    cored and each cut into 8 wedges
salt and freshly ground pepper
1/2 cup crumbled Gorgonzola cheese
1/4 cup toasted walnuts

• Prepare a grill for barbecue. Oil the grill rack. Lay the radicchio wedges on a foil-lined baking sheet and brush with the olive oil. Season lightly with salt and pepper. Grill over medium-high heat for 15 minutes, or until crisp around the edges and just tender. Place on a platter and sprinkle with the cheese and walnuts. Drizzle with olive oil and serve at once.

PER SERVING: 335 CALORIES; 11 G PROTEIN; 9 G CARBOHYDRATES;
29 G TOTAL FAT; 8 G SATURATED FAT; 32 MG CHOLESTEROL; 823 MG SODIUM

COOKS' TIP:

Makes sure your cheese is at room temperature so it will melt onto the hot radicchio.

Soy-Glazed Okra

MAKES 4 SERVINGS

This delicious Japanese version of cooking the beautiful but much maligned okra pods will have even kids asking for more. The glaze is not the only reason: grilling changes the gooey interior so there are only crisp-tender green seeds inside.

oil for grill
1/4 cup plus 2 tablespoons low-sodium soy sauce
11/2 tablespoons honey
11/2 tablespoons sherry or dry white wine
11/2 teaspoons grated peeled fresh gingerroot
2 small garlic cloves, crushed through a press
1/2 teaspoon Asian sesame oil
1 pound okra, stem end trimmed but not cut off

• Prepare a grill for barbecue. Soak eight thin wooden skewers in hot water. Oil the grill rack. In a medium bowl, whisk the soy sauce with the honey, sherry, gingerroot, garlic, and sesame oil. Add the okra and toss to coat. Working on a foil-lined baking sheet, double-skewer the okra with the like ends facing the same way. Grill over hot heat for 4 minutes, turning once, until okra is tender and browned.

PER SERVING: 81 CALORIES; 3 G PROTEIN; 17 G CARBOHYDRATES; 1 G TOTAL
FAT; 0 G SATURATED FAT; 0 MG CHOLESTEROL; 947 MG SODIUM

Tomato, Leek, and Fennel Packets

MAKES 4 SERVINGS

You can use the last of the coals to grill vegetables for another day. Make up these packets hours ahead of dinner and give the leeks and fennel a second cooking alongside steaks or fish fillets.

1/4 cup extra virgin olive oil, plus extra for the grill

1 large fennel bulb

4 thin leeks, trimmed with layers at root end intact,
*   white and tender yellow-green portions only*

salt and freshly ground pepper

16 red grape or small pear tomatoes

16 yellow grape or small yellow pear tomatoes

1/4 cup bottled Dijon vinaigrette dressing

2 tablespoons chopped fennel fern

● Prepare a grill for barbecue. Oil the grill rack. Cut the fennel bulb into 8 slices through the root, keeping the layers of the slices intact. Split the leeks in half lengthwise and rinse well. Place the fennel and leeks on a foil-lined baking sheet and brush on each side with the olive oil; sprinkle with salt and pepper.

● Grill the fennel and leeks over medium-high heat about 4 minutes on each side, until lightly charred and tender. Remove the fennel from the grill and place on a plate. Place the leeks together in a line on a cutting board and cut crosswise into 1-inch pieces, keeping the leeks separate so they can be portioned out leek by leek.

● Stack 8 sections of heavy-duty aluminum foil (each 12 inches long) on the work surface. Place 2 fennel wedges, 1 leek, 4 of each color tomato, 1 tablespoon dressing, and 1/4 of the fennel fern on top; season with a pinch of salt and pepper, and fold up 2 pieces of foil (to make a double thickness) around the mixture. Seal tightly and move to the side. Repeat with remaining foil, vegetables, dressing, fern, salt, and pepper to make 4 packets.

● Grill packets over medium-high heat until you can hear the juices boiling, 5 to 7 minutes. Be cautious opening the hot packets to avoid the hot steam and serve from the foil.

PER SERVING: 290 CALORIES; 3 G PROTEIN; 24 G CARBOHYDRATES;
22 G TOTAL FAT; 3 G SATURATED FAT; 0 MG CHOLESTEROL; 61 MG SODIUM

COOKS' TIP:

Any mix of vegetables will go well with the tomatoes and seasoning. You can even make one big packet and bring it to the table to serve family-style.

Grilled Green Tomatoes

MAKES 4 SERVINGS

Enjoy this dish in early summer, when green tomatoes are readily available.

1/4 cup grapeseed oil

1/2 teaspoon Tabasco sauce

1/2 cup coarse yellow cornmeal

1/2 teaspoon salt

2 medium green tomatoes, cut crosswise into
   3/4-inch-thick slices

• Prepare a grill for barbecue. Oil the grill rack and a vegetable grilling pan; set the pan on the grill to preheat.

• Place the grapeseed oil in a shallow bowl and stir in the Tabasco. Mix the cornmeal and salt in another bowl. Spread out tomatoes on a foil-lined baking sheet; brush on both sides with the oil mixture. Dip one side of each tomato in the cornmeal mixture and shake off excess. Press mixture gently onto tomato. Grill tomatoes in preheated pan over high heat for about 1 1/2 minutes, or until heated through and lightly charred. Turn tomatoes over and grill 30 seconds.

PER SERVING: 202 CALORIES; 2 G PROTEIN; 27 G CARBOHYDRATES;
22 G TOTAL FAT; 2 G SATURATED FAT; 0 MG CHOLESTEROL; 301 MG SODIUM

COOKS' TIP:

Sweet, tender, green heirloom tomatoes are not the same as hard, tart, green, unripened red tomatoes, so grill the former for best results.

Grilled Japanese Eggplants

MAKES 8 SERVINGS

These are good with a cooling yogurt sauce.

1/4 cup extra virgin olive oil plus extra for the grill

2 tablespoons rice vinegar

1 tablespoon soy sauce

1/2 teaspoon hot Maryland-style seafood spice mix

4 Japanese eggplants (6 ounces each), halved
   lengthwise

Gomashio (Japanese sesame-seed salt, recipe on
   page 219)

• Prepare a grill for barbecue. Oil the grill rack. Mix the oil, vinegar, soy sauce, and spice mix in a bowl. Score (about 1/8-inch deep) the cut sides of the eggplants in a crosshatch pattern and place on a baking sheet. Brush the oil mixture over the cut sides and let marinate at least 15 minutes. Grill the eggplants, cut sides down first, over medium heat for about 10 minutes, turning once, until tender and browned. Sprinkle the cut sides with gomashio. Cut crosswise into 1-inch diagonal pieces.

PER SERVING: 89 CALORIES; 1 G PROTEIN; 6 G CARBOHYDRATES; 7 G TOTAL
FAT; 1 G SATURATED FAT; 0 MG CHOLESTEROL; 132 MG SODIUM

PREP TIME: 10 MINUTES   COOKING TIME: 12 MINUTES

Mixed-Vegetable Skewers

MAKES 4 SERVINGS

You can put kids or guests to work assembling these while you do something else. If your tomatoes are very ripe, skewer them separately, and cook them just until charred and hot or they will explode.

8 yellow baby pattypan squash (about 8 ounces total)
8 green baby pattypan squash (about 8 ounces total)
8 red pearl onions or shallots (about 8 ounces total)
8 red cherry tomatoes
8 yellow cherry tomatoes
8 small tomatillos
1/3 cup bottled Caesar salad dressing

● Prepare a grill for barbecue. Onto four 14-inch-long metal skewers, tightly thread the pattypans, pearl onions, tomatoes, and tomatillos in an alternating pattern. Brush the skewers with some of the dressing.

● Grill the skewers over a medium-hot fire, turning frequently, until the vegetables are lightly charred and barely tender, about 12 minutes.

● Slide the vegetables off the skewers and onto plates. Drizzle with the remaining dressing.

PER SERVING: 191 CALORIES; 5 G PROTEIN; 24 G CARBOHYDRATES; 10 G TOTAL FAT; 2 G SATURATED FAT; 0 MG CHOLESTEROL; 187 MG SODIUM

COOKS' TIP:

You can use any flavor dressing or homemade dressing, but one with herbs and garlic is ideal.

Grilled Portobellos with Cilantro Cream Sauce

MAKES 4 SERVINGS

These meaty mushrooms are ideal as a replacement for the meat dish when serving the vegetarians at the table, but other diners will find them perfect alongside a steak or burger.

2 tablespoons extra virgin olive oil plus extra for
    the grill
4 portobello mushrooms, stems removed, caps wiped
    clean of any soil
salt and pepper

CILANTRO CREAM SAUCE
1 cup sour cream
1/2 cup milk
1/2 cup finely chopped cilantro
2 teaspoons fresh lime juice
salt and freshly ground pepper to taste

COOKS' TIP:

The flavorful sauce is also delicious swirled into soup, poured over a platter of grilled fish, or whisked into mashed potatoes.

- Prepare a grill for barbecuing. Oil the grill rack. Place the mushrooms on a foil-lined baking sheet and brush on both sides with olive oil. Season with salt and pepper and grill rounded sides up over medium heat 8 minutes. Brush rounded side of caps with oil and turn over. Grill until tender, about 7 minutes longer.

- While mushrooms cook, make the Cilantro Cream Sauce: In a small bowl, blend the sour cream with the milk, cilantro, and lime juice and season with salt and pepper.

- Place the mushrooms rounded side up on a cutting board and slice into 1/4-inch-wide slices. Fan out slices slightly but keeping caps together on four individual plates or on a platter and drizzle the sauce on top. Serve immediately.

MUSHROOMS ONLY, PER SERVING: 88 CALORIES; 3 G PROTEIN;
5 G CARBOHYDRATES; 7 G TOTAL FAT; 1 G SATURATED FAT; 0 MG CHOLESTEROL;
6 MG SODIUM
CILANTRO CREAM SAUCE, PER SERVING: 125 CALORIES; 3 G PROTEIN;
4 G CARBOHYDRATES; 11 G TOTAL FAT; 7 G SATURATED FAT;
25 MG CHOLESTEROL; 623 MG SODIUM

PREP TIME: 10 MINUTES   COOKING TIME: 31 MINUTES

Grilled Belgian Endive with Roquefort Sauce

MAKES 4 SERVINGS

Raw or cooked, the bitter, juicy leaves of Belgian endive are wonderfully matched to sweet, salty blue cheeses, especially Roquefort. If you want, sprinkle some toasted hazelnuts or almonds over each portion.

olive oil for brushing
4 heads Belgian endive
salt and freshly ground pepper
1 tablespoon coarsely chopped flat-leaf parsley

ROQUEFORT SAUCE
3 tablespoons unsalted butter
1 shallot, minced
salt and freshly ground pepper
1/2 cup dry white wine
3/4 cup heavy cream
1/4 cup crumbled Roquefort cheese (about 2 ounces)
1/2 teaspoon finely chopped rosemary

• Prepare a grill for barbecuing. Oil a grill rack.

• Make the Roquefort Sauce: Melt the butter in a large, deep skillet. Add the shallot, season with salt and pepper, and cook over medium-high heat, stirring frequently, until the shallot is softened, about 3 minutes. Add the wine and simmer until reduced to 2 table-spoons, about 5 minutes. Add the cream, Roquefort, and rosemary and simmer over moderately low heat until slightly thickened, about 7 minutes; keep warm.

• Rinse the endives and pat dry. Cut in half lengthwise and place on a foil-lined baking sheet. Brush with oil and sprinkle with salt and pepper. Grill cut side down over medium-high heat 7 minutes; turn over with tongs and grill until tender and browned, about 7 minutes longer. Place endive halves cut sides up on a platter; spoon sauce over each endive. Sprinkle with parsley before serving.

ENDIVES ONLY, PER SERVING: 41 CALORIES; 1 G PROTEIN;
2 G CARBOHYDRATES; 4 G TOTAL FAT; 0 G SATURATED FAT; 0 MG CHOLESTEROL;
290 MG SODIUM
ROQUEFORT SAUCE, PER SERVING: 212 CALORIES; 5 G PROTEIN;
4 G CARBOHYDRATES; 18 G TOTAL FAT; 11 G SATURATED FAT;
53 MG CHOLESTEROL; 424 MG SODIUM

COOKS' TIP:

If you're short on time, you can use a good bottled blue cheese dressing instead of making the sauce.

PREP TIME: 5 MINUTES   COOKING TIME: 55 MINUTES

Basic Roasted Garlic

MAKES 24 SERVINGS

With roasting, garlic makes a transformation from pungent and sharp to pungent and sweet. The creamy cooked cloves are as versatile as the raw ones, but the altered personality invites the cook into uncharted territory, begging to be mashed into dishes to which no one in his right mind would add the raw stuff.

4 heads garlic
1/4 cup olive oil

- Prepare a grill for barbecuing. Place garlic heads on squares of heavy-duty aluminum foil and brush generously with oil. Fold up foil to seal garlic packets tightly; place over medium coals and roast 45 to 55 minutes, until tender when pierced with a paring knife, testing after 20 minutes to make sure the heat is right so the garlic is not burning. Remove packets from the heat and let cool completely before opening. Reserve any juices for use in a recipe. To use, separate garlic cloves and snip off the tip of each clove with kitchen shears. Squeeze out roasted garlic clove into a bowl.

PER SERVING: 9 CALORIES; 0 G PROTEIN; 2 G CARBOHYDRATES;
0 G TOTAL FAT; 0 MG CHOLESTEROL; 1 MG SODIUM

COOKS' TIP:

Roasted garlic freezes well, but you will want to separate the cloves so you can remove only what you need to use at one time.

PREP TIME: 15 MINUTES   COOKING TIME: 15 MINUTES

Grilled Onions and Polenta

MAKES 4 SERVINGS

You can find tubes of cooked polenta in the produce department of even small grocery stores. If you make your own polenta, pour it into a cake pan and let it cool. Refrigerate it until firm, invert it onto a cutting board, and cut it into 3½-inch rounds or rounds the diameter of your onions.

extra virgin olive oil

2 red onions, peeled

4 rounds (½-inch thick) store-bought polenta, plain or flavored

¼ cup bottled red-wine vinaigrette dressing

½ cup chopped plum tomatoes, seeded

¼ cup finely snipped fresh chives

salt and freshly ground pepper

• Prepare a grill for barbecue. Oil the grill rack. Soak four thin wooden skewers in hot water.

• Cut the onions crosswise into ½-inch-thick slices. Reserve the 4 center slices and use the remainder for something else. Insert a skewer horizontally through each onion slice to keep the rings together. Place polenta and onions on a foil-lined baking sheet and brush on both sides with dressing. Grill on grilling tray over medium-low heat turning once, until onions are caramelized and tender and polenta crust is crisp, about 15 minutes.

• Place each onion slice on a polenta round and transfer to 4 plates. Sprinkle with tomatoes, chives, salt, and pepper and drizzle with oil.

PER SERVING: 166 CALORIES; 3 G PROTEIN; 23 G CARBOHYDRATES; 7 G TOTAL FAT; 1 G SATURATED FAT; 0 MG CHOLESTEROL; 718 MG SODIUM

COOKS' TIP:

You can grill a few mushrooms on skewers alongside the onions, slice them thinly, and sprinkle them over the onions.

PREP TIME: 15 MINUTES   COOKING TIME: 4 MINUTES

Miso-Glazed Tofu and Vegetable Kebabs with Ginger-Miso Dipping Sauce

MAKES 4 SERVINGS

The fermented soybean paste called miso comes in many flavors, and the yellow is the mildest and most versatile. It caramelizes as it grills and adds a tangy "meatiness" to the tofu.

1 package (15 ounces) firm tofu, drained and
*   patted dry*
1/3 cup yellow miso
3 tablespoons sake or beer
1 1/2 tablespoons Asian sesame oil
1 tablespoon tomato paste
1 teaspoon Chinese chile-garlic paste
8 fresh wide-cap shiitake or 1-inch button mushrooms
8 snow peas, ends trimmed, strings removed
2 large scallions, trimmed to light green and white
*   portions only, cut into 2-inch lengths*
2 tablespoons toasted sesame seeds
Ginger-Miso Dipping Sauce, recipe follows
seasoned or plain nori (Japanese seaweed), cut into
*   3-inch squares, for serving (optional)*

• Prepare a grill for barbecue. Soak 16 thin wooden skewers in hot water. Layer 3 paper towels in a shallow baking dish and place the tofu on top. Set another baking dish on top and add two 1-pound cans of anything to weight the tofu. Let tofu stand 10 minutes to drain, then remove to a cutting board and slice into 1-inch cubes.

• Prepare the miso glaze: In a small bowl, mix the miso, sake, oil, tomato paste, and chile-garlic paste.

• Remove stems from the shiitakes or trim a thin slice from the ends of the button mushrooms. Double-skewer (parallel, about 1/4 inch apart, in the center) the tofu cubes, mushrooms, snow peas, and scallions, alternating ingredients and threading shiitake caps and snowpeas twice onto the skewers so they will lie more or less flat on the grill. Place kebabs on a foil-lined baking sheet and brush with miso glaze.

• Cook kebabs over hot heat 4 minutes, turning every minute and basting with remaining miso glaze, until tofu is browned and vegetables are cooked through. Arrrange kebabs on a platter and sprinkle with sesame seeds. Serve with Ginger-Miso Dipping Sauce and nori, if you like.

KEBABS ONLY, PER SERVING: 279 CALORIES; 15 G PROTEIN;
35 G CARBOHYDRATES; 12 G TOTAL FAT; 1 G SATURATED FAT;
0 MG CHOLESTEROL; 891 MG SODIUM

Ginger-Miso Dipping Sauce

MAKES 4 SERVINGS, ABOUT 3/4 CUP

This is a versatile sauce. Use as a dipping sauce for vegetables or boiled shrimp. Serve with poached or grilled salmon or tuna. Toss with cold soba noodles, steamed broccoli, or snow peas. Drizzle over grilled chicken breasts or pork tenderloin.

1 slice of peeled fresh gingerroot (3/4-inch thick), grated on a microplane
2 tablespoons shredded carrot
2 tablespoons fresh lime juice
1 tablespoon low-sodium soy sauce
1 teaspoon miso paste
1/4 teaspoon crushed red pepper flakes
1/2 cup ginger ale or water

• Combine the gingerroot, carrot, lime juice, soy sauce, miso, and pepper flakes in a small bowl and whisk until smooth. Whisk in the ginger ale.

PER SERVING: 19 CALORIES; 0 G PROTEIN; 4 G CARBOHYDRATES; 0 G TOTAL FAT; 0 MG CHOLESTEROL; 141 MG SODIUM

COOKS' TIP:

Fresh ginger is so good for you! Peel and slice the remainder and use it for making tea or in chicken stock.

Grilled-Chayote Pizzas

MAKES 4 SERVINGS

Peel this pear-shaped gourd and remove the seed; you'll soon be eating one of the main foods of the Mayans and Aztecs. The mild flavor makes it a happy partner to any mix of spices. Try it raw in a salad or baked like acorn squash.

olive oil for brushing
1 pound frozen pizza dough, thawed, recipe follows
1 large chayote (3/4 pound), halved lengthwise, pitted and cut lengthwise into 24 slices
1 red onion, thinly sliced
salt and freshly ground pepper
1 teaspoon ground cumin
vegetable oil for the grill
2 cups shredded Monterey Jack cheese with jalapeños

• Prepare a grill for barbecuing. Place a vegetable grilling pan on the grill to preheat. Brush two baking sheets with olive oil. On a lightly floured work surface, roll out one-half of dough to an 8-inch round about 1/4-inch thick and place on a prepared baking sheet. Repeat with remaining dough.

• Place chayote and onion slices on a foil-lined baking sheet and brush on both sides with olive oil. Sprinkle with salt, pepper, and cumin. In 2 batches, grill the chayote and onion in the grill pan over medium-hot coals until lightly charred, turning once, about 2 minutes each side. Remove to the foil-lined baking sheet and fold up foil to keep mixture warm.

● Brush the grill with vegetable oil. Brush the dough rounds on both sides with olive oil. Place the dough rounds and filling near the grill. Grill dough rounds over medium-low heat 2 to 3 minutes on one side, until lightly charred and barely crisp. Turn rounds over and sprinkle with the cheese. Top with the chayote and onion and grill until the cheese melts, about 3 more minutes, moving pizzas to a cooler region of the grill if needed to keep the dough from burning. Slide pizzas onto a wooden cutting board and serve.

PER SERVING: 436 CALORIES; 20 G PROTEIN; 42 G CARBOHYDRATES; 21 G TOTAL FAT; 11 G SATURATED FAT; 50 MG CHOLESTEROL; 741 MG SODIUM

COOKS' TIPS:

● If you can't find chayote (look for it in Hispanic grocery stores), use summer squash or zucchini.

● To thaw 1 pound of frozen pizza dough quickly, place dough on a microwave-safe plate and brush lightly with olive oil. Cover with plastic wrap and microwave on HIGH power in 20-second increments, turning dough over each time, until softened but not hot. When dough has thawed enough to cut, cut it into 4 pieces and thaw at 10-second increments until dough can be rolled.

PREP TIME: 20 MINUTES PLUS RISING

Homemade Pizza Dough

MAKES 4 DOUGH BALLS

If you make this dough once, you'll make it time and time again. And for dieters, note that homemade dough has lots fewer carbs than a store-bought one.

2/3 cup lukewarm water (105° to 115° F)
2 teaspoons active dry yeast
1 1/3 cups all-purpose flour, plus additional if needed, and for dusting
1 tablespoon sugar
pinch of salt
olive oil for brushing

● In a medium bowl, mix the water with the yeast and 1 teaspoon flour until yeast is dissolved. Add the sugar and salt and stir to dissolve. Stir in the flour and turn out dough onto a floured work surface. Knead dough until smooth. Clean out and lightly oil the bowl. Add the dough and turn over so it is lightly oiled on all sides. Cover with plastic wrap and let rise in a warm place until doubled in bulk, about 1 hour.

● Punch down dough and form it into four balls. Use for pizzas, calzones, or flat breads.

PER DOUGH BALL: 197 CALORIES; 5 G PROTEIN; 35 G CARBOHYDRATES; 4 G TOTAL FAT; 0 G SATURATED FAT; 0 MG CHOLESTEROL; 146 MG SODIUM

Feta and Eggplant Pita Pizzas

MAKES 8 PIZZAS

Without a dough to make, these appetizers couldn't be easier to prepare. Have all your ingredients ready ahead of time, then grill the eggplant slices when the flames subside on the newly made fire. (Not too close to the hot coals or the eggplant will burn.) Your guests can eat the pizzas while the main course is cooking.

1 large eggplant
4 pita breads (4 inches in diameter)
1 jar (6 1/2 ounces) marinated artichokes
4 ounces feta cheese, finely crumbled
1/4 cup sliced black olives
1/2 teaspoon dried oregano leaves
pinch of cayenne
freshly ground black pepper

• Prepare a grill for barbecuing. Using a vegetable peeler, peel off wide lengthwise strips of eggplant so there will be alternate strips of peeled and unpeeled eggplant. Cut eggplant crosswise to make 8 slices the diameter of the pita breads and place on a foil-lined baking sheet. Reserve remaining eggplant for another use.

• Using kitchen shears, cut pitas in half around the curve to make 8 rounds and place on another foil-lined baking sheet. Drain marinade from artichoke hearts into a bowl and brush marinade on both sides of eggplant slices and pita halves. Place artichokes in the bowl and snip with shears into bite-size pieces. Add cheese, olives, oregano, cayenne, and black pepper and mix well.

• Grill eggplant slices 1 minute on both sides or until lightly browned. Remove to foil-lined baking sheet. Grill pitas on cut sides until lightly toasted and remove to foil-lined baking sheet. Top each pita with an eggplant slice and then 1/8 of the feta mixture. Spread mixture evenly. Grill pizzas 2 minutes, until heated through.

PER SERVING: 96 CALORIES; 4 G PROTEIN; 13 G CARBOHYDRATES; 5 G TOTAL FAT; 2 G SATURATED FAT; 13 MG CHOLESTEROL; 327 MG SODIUM

PREP TIME: 25 MINUTES   COOKING TIME: 37 MINUTES

Fire-Roasted Tomato Soup with Grilled-Tomatillo Cream

MAKES 6 SERVINGS

The roasted flavors of tomatoes, tomatillos, and garlic add a depth and complexity to this soup. The tangy crème fraîche and lime juice swirl is also good in a roasted corn chowder.

1/2 *pound tomatillos, husked*
2 *pounds firm ripe tomatoes*
vegetable oil for brushing
1 *bunch scallions*
2 *yellow or white corn tortillas (6 inches in diameter)*
salt and freshly ground pepper
1/4 *teaspoon ground cumin*
1/4 *teaspoon ground coriander*
1 *cup cilantro leaves*
1/3 *cup crème fraîche or sour cream*
2 *tablespoons fresh lime juice*
3 *large roasted garlic cloves (recipe, page 165)*
2 *cups vegetable stock*
lime wedges and green hot sauce, for serving

● Prepare a grill for barbecuing. Place the tomatillos and tomatoes on a foil-lined baking sheet and brush with oil. Grill over medium-high heat until charred, turning, 10 to 15 minutes. Remove to a bowl and cool slightly.

● Oil the grill rack. Place scallions and tortillas on a foil-lined baking sheet, brush with oil and sprinkle scallions with salt, pepper, cumin, and coriander.

● Grill scallions perpendicular to the grill rack so they won't fall through, and grill until charred, about 10 minutes, turning once. Remove to a cutting board, remove badly charred portions, and cut the remainder crosswise into 1/4-inch pieces. Set aside. Grill the tortillas until charred and crisp, turning once, about 2 minutes in all. Remove to a cutting board and crush lightly into bite-size pieces. Set aside.

● Prepare tomatillo cream: In a blender or food processor, combine the tomatillos with 1/4 cup of the cilantro leaves, the crème fraîche, and lime juice and blend until puréed. Transfer to a small bowl and season with salt and pepper. Set aside.

● Using a food mill, purée the tomatoes and roasted garlic into a saucepan and discard the skins and seeds. Add the stock and scallions, season with salt and pepper, and bring to a boil. Reduce the heat to medium-low and simmer for 10 minutes, stirring occasionally.

● To serve: Ladle the soup into bowls and swirl in the tomatillo cream. Sprinkle with the remaining cilantro and tortillas. Pass the lime wedges and hot sauce.

PER SERVING: 101 CALORIES; 14 G PROTEIN; 15 G CARBOHYDRATES; 13 G TOTAL FAT; 3 G SATURATED FAT; 9 MG CHOLESTEROL; 836 MG SODIUM

PREP TIME: 25 MINUTES   COOKING TIME: 11 MINUTES

Roasted Corn on the Cob with Ancho Butter and Cheese

MAKES 4 SERVINGS

Grilled corn is sold as street food all over the world. The sight, sound, and aroma of corn grilling over a fire always draws a crowd of hungry snackers, so you may want to serve this as an appetizer rather than as an accompaniment to the entrée.

4 ears of corn, shucked
1/2 cup freshly grated Cotija cheese (available in Mexican grocery stores) or Pecorino Romano cheese
lime wedges for serving

ANCHO BUTTER
11/4 teaspoons ground coriander
1 teaspoon ancho chile powder
1/4 teaspoon ground cumin
1 clove roasted garlic (recipe, page 165)
1 stick (4 ounces) unsalted butter, softened

- Soak the corn in a pot of cold water at least 20 minutes or overnight, in the refrigerator. About 20 minutes before cooking, prepare a grill for barbecuing.

- Prepare the Ancho Butter: In a small nonstick skillet, heat the coriander, chile powder, and cumin over medium heat, stirring, until fragrant, about 3 minutes, and place in a food processor. Squeeze the garlic pulp from the skin into the food processor and add the butter. Process until smooth and scrape out into a serving bowl.

- Drain the corn and grill over high heat 6 to 8 minutes, turning every 2 minutes to brown it evenly. Remove the corn to plates. To serve, slather corn with Ancho Butter and sprinkle with cheese. Pass lime wedges for squeezing onto the corn as desired.

CORN, CHEESE, AND LIME ONLY, PER SERVING: 192 CALORIES; 10 G PROTEIN; 31 G CARBOHYDRATES; 6 G TOTAL FAT; 3 G SATURATED FAT; 15 MG CHOLESTEROL; 193 MG SODIUM
ANCHO BUTTER, PER SERVING: 104 CALORIES; 0 G PROTEIN; 0 G CARBOHYDRATES; 12 G TOTAL FAT; 7 G SATURATED FAT; 31 MG CHOLESTEROL; 6 MG SODIUM

PREP TIME: 15 MINUTES   COOKING TIME: 12 MINUTES

Tahini-Glazed Tofu "Burgers"

MAKES 4 SERVINGS

Tofu is so wonderful grilled that even "tofuphobics" will eat it. Grilled tofu is a popular street food in Japan.

1 package (15 ounces) firm tofu, drained and
    patted dry
2 tablespoons extra virgin olive oil, plus extra
    for the grill
salt and freshly ground pepper
1/2 cup tahini, at room temperature
1 tablespoon honey
2 teaspoons fresh lemon juice
1 large garlic clove, crushed through a press
4 scallions, white and light green parts only,
    thinly sliced
lemon wedges, for serving

COOKS' TIP:

Tahini is a thick paste made from sesame seeds. You can find it most grocery stores, but certainly in health food stores and Middle Eastern grocery stores.

● Prepare a grill for barbecue. Layer three paper towels in a shallow baking dish and place the tofu on top. Set another baking dish on top and add two 1-pound cans of anything to weight the tofu. Let tofu stand 10 minutes to drain, then remove to a cutting board and slice horizontally in half. Cut crosswise in half.

● Oil the grill rack. Place the tofu slices in a hinged grill rack on a foil-lined baking sheet, brush tofu on both sides with 1 tablespoon of the olive oil and season with salt and pepper. Grill over medium heat for about 10 minutes, turning once, until tender and browned.

● Meanwhile, in a small bowl, whisk the tahini with the honey, lemon juice, garlic, and the remaining 1 tablespoon of olive oil. Season with salt and pepper. Spread the tahini sauce over the tofu slices, turn the slices over, and grill 1 minute on each side, until the tahini sauce is browned. Sprinkle with the scallions and serve at once with lemon wedges.

PER SERVING: 347 CALORIES; 15 G PROTEIN; 21 G CARBOHYDRATES; 26 G TOTAL FAT; 3 G SATURATED FAT; 0 MG CHOLESTEROL; 325 MG SODIUM

PREP TIME: 30 MINUTES   COOKING TIME: 8 MINUTES

Garlic Potato Cakes
with Olive-Almond Butter

MAKES 4 SERVINGS

extra virgin olive oil for brushing
2 cups mashed potatoes, made with butter and salt
2 large garlic cloves, crushed through a press
2 tablespoons finely snipped fresh chives
salt and freshly ground pepper to taste
Olive-Almond Butter, recipe follows

● Prepare a grill for barbecuing. Place a hinged burger grilling rack on a foil-lined baking sheet and brush grill with oil. Mix the mashed potatoes with the garlic and chives in a bowl. Taste and adjust the salt and pepper if needed. Shape into 4 patties about 3/4-inch thick, and brush on both sides with olive oil. Place on burger grill, close grill, and secure.

● Grill the potato cakes 6 inches over medium-hot coals until browned and crisp on both sides, and piping hot on the inside, about 4 minutes per side, turning every 2 minutes. Serve topped with a thin slice of Olive-Almond Butter.

Olive-Almond Butter

Serve to top grilled fish, meats, poultry, and vegetables. Add a dollop to soups or spread on toasted breads as a base for bruschetta.

1 stick unsalted butter, softened
1/4 cup chopped almond-stuffed olives
1 tablespoon finely chopped fresh thyme leaves,
   without stems

● Combine butter with chopped olives and thyme in a medium bowl and stir until well blended. Mound along the length in the center of a 10-inch piece of waxed paper and join the edges of the long sides. Press the paper over the butter and shape into a cylinder. Roll up the cylinder and twist the short ends. Refrigerate or freeze to set the butter.

● To serve, unwrap the butter and cut crosswise into rounds.

POTATO CAKE, PER SERVING: 102 CALORIES; 3 G PROTEIN; 20 G CARBOHYDRATES;
2 G TOTAL FAT; 1 G SATURATED FAT; 2 MG CHOLESTEROL; 273 MG SODIUM
OLIVE-ALMOND BUTTER, PER TABLESPOON: 115 CALORIES; 1 G PROTEIN;
1 G CARBOHYDRATES; 13 G TOTAL FAT; 7 G SATURATED FAT;
31 MG CHOLESTEROL; 39 MG SODIUM

Desserts

Gingerbread Kebabs •

Grilled 3-Plum Tarts •

Mini Truffle S'mores •

Rum-Basted Fruit Kebabs •

Grilled Stuffed Figs •

Vanilla-Sugared Apricots •

Grilled Butterscotch Pineapple •

Nutty Bananas •

• Bartlett Pears with Chocolate Sauce

• Grilled Cheese Blintzes

• Grilled Peach Melba Sundaes

• Spiced Pink Grapefruit

• Toasted Cake and Berries
  with Goat Cheese Cream

• Grilled Ambrosia

• Rocky Road Crêpe Torte

PREP TIME: 15 MINUTES   COOKING TIME: 10 MINUTES

Gingerbread Kebabs

MAKES 4 SERVINGS

Bring a touch of Christmas to the summer backyard feast with the addition of spicy gingerbread.

1 loaf gingerbread, store-bought or homemade

1/2 cup orange marmalade

8 unhulled strawberries

2 kiwifruit, peeled and quartered lengthwise

2 slices (1-inch thick) fresh pineapple, cored and
    cut into 12 chunks

oil for the grill

COOKS' TIP:

You can use any kind of nut bread instead of the gingerbread.

• Prepare a grill for barbecuing. Soak eight wooden skewers in hot water. Cut the gingerbread into 12 one-inch cubes. Heat the marmalade in the microwave or in a saucepan until melted.

• Working on a foil-lined baking sheet, double-skewer the gingerbread cubes alternating with the strawberries, kiwi, and pineapple. Brush with marmalade.

• Oil the grill. Grill the kebabs over medium-high heat until gingerbread and fruit are hot, about 8 minutes, turning every 2 minutes.

PER SERVING: 433 CALORIES; 4 G PROTEIN; 81 G CARBOHYDRATES; 13 G TOTAL FAT; 3 G SATURATED FAT; 24 MG CHOLESTEROL; 267 MG SODIUM

PREP TIME: 20 MINUTES   COOKING TIME: 28 MINUTES

Grilled 3-Plum Tarts

MAKES 4 SERVINGS

Some folks like tart plums; others like them sweet. Grilling concentrates their fruit juices and caramelizes them, so everyone will be happy as they savor their assorted colors and flavors on crunchy pastry spread with lemon curd.

1 sheet frozen all-butter puff pastry, thawed

2 ripe black plums, halved, pitted

2 ripe red plums, halved, pitted

2 ripe green plums, halved, pitted

grapeseed oil

3 tablespoons cinnamon sugar

3/4 cup store-bought or homemade lemon curd

COOKS' TIP:

You can omit the pastry and just serve the plum slices in a compote dish with a dollop of the lemon curd or lemon gelato.

● Preheat the oven to 425° F. Roll the puff pastry 1/8-inch thick. Prick the pastry with a fork. Cut into 5- or 6-inch rounds and place on a parchment-lined baking sheet. Cover with another sheet of parchment and another baking sheet. Bake for 20 to 25 minutes, or until golden and crisp. Remove the baking sheet and the top layer of parchment. Let the pastry cool on the baking sheet on a wire rack.

● Prepare a grill for barbecuing. Place fruit on a foil-lined baking sheet. Lightly oil the cut sides of the plums and the grill.

● Grill the plums, cut sides down, 1 minute. Turn the plums over and grill 45 seconds longer. Spoon cinnamon sugar onto cut sides of plums and pat onto the fruit with the back of a spoon. Turn plums, sugared side down, and grill 30 seconds longer to caramelize the sugar.

● Remove the plums to a cutting board and when they are cool enough to handle, remove the skins if they are loose. Cut each half into 4 wedges with a sharp knife. Spread the lemon curd over the pastry rounds and arrange the plums, cut sides up, in a pinwheel design alternating the colors of the plums.

PER SERVING: 548 CALORIES; 6 G PROTEIN; 62 G CARBOHYDRATES; 32 G FAT; 19 G SATURATED FAT; 184 G CHOLESTEROL; 586 MG SODIUM

Mini Truffle S'mores

MAKES 4 SERVINGS

These bites are all you need to finish a grilled meal. The warmed cookies help to melt the truffles and hot marshmallows complete the sweet sandwich in classic gooey style.

16 chocolate wafer cookies
8 chocolate truffle candies, diced
8 marshmallows

• Prepare a grill for barbecuing. Place half the cookies, flat side up, on a foil-lined baking sheet that is small enough to fit on the grill. Top with pieces of truffle. Place the baking sheet on the grill.

• Thread the marshmallows on skewers and grill until soft and charred. Place one hot marshmallow on each truffle-sprinkled cookie and top with a plain cookie, flat side down. Press lightly.

PER SERVING: 230 CALORIES; 2 G PROTEIN; 47 G CARBOHYDRATES;
6 G TOTAL FAT; 2 G SATURATED FAT; 1 MG CHOLESTEROL; 152 MG SODIUM

COOKS' TIP:

You can sprinkle chocolate chips on the cookies—or any other wafer cookies—instead of using truffle candy.

Rum-Basted Fruit Kebabs

MAKES 4 SERVINGS

You may never go back to pie à la mode after ending a meal with these beautiful, refreshing kebabs. The variety of fruit combinations is endless, but you'll want to include dazzling starfruit every time.

4 tablespoons unsalted butter

1/2 cup spiced rum

1/2 cup light brown sugar

11/2 teaspoons cinnamon

16 chunks (3/4-inch thick) fresh pineapple

16 pieces (3/4-inch thick) firm finger bananas

8 red grapes

8 black grapes

4 crosswise slices (1/2-inch thick) starfruit

● Prepare a grill for barbecuing. In a small saucepan, melt the butter over high heat until lightly browned, 1 to 2 minutes. Add the rum and heat just until boiling. Stir in the brown sugar and cinnamon. Remove pan from the heat. Arrange fruit in alternate slices on skewers, making sure the starfruit is skewered through the skin. Place skewers on a foil-lined baking sheet and brush on all sides with rum mixture. Grill over hot coals 2 minutes, turning once.

PER SERVING: 344 CALORIES; 1 G PROTEIN; 45 G CARBOHYDRATES; 12 G TOTAL FAT; 7 G SATURATED FAT; 31 MG CHOLESTEROL; 11 MG SODIUM

COOKS' TIP:

Using spiced rum is a shortcut to seasoning the fruit, but you can omit it and use orange juice, 1/4 teaspoon cinnamon, and a pinch of allspice instead.

Grilled Stuffed Figs

MAKES 4 SERVINGS

Those who say they only eat figs fresh are missing out on the only other way figs "should" be eaten: grilled. The sweet caramelized flesh is decadent with the melted creamy cheese.

4 ounces triple-crème soft ripened cheese such
*   as Explorateur*
4 fresh black figs
4 fresh green figs
grapeseed oil for brushing figs

• Prepare a grill for barbecuing. Cut the cheese into sixteen 1/2-inch slivers, a little shorter than the height of the figs. Working on a foil-lined baking sheet, make a slit in the top of the figs and stuff 2 slices of cheese into each. Brush figs lightly with oil.

• Oil the grill. Grill figs over medium-high heat first on their sides and then upright for 8 to 10 minutes total, until the cheese is melted and the figs are warm.

PER SERVING: 238 CALORIES; 4 G PROTEIN; 29 G CARBOHYDRATES;
14 G TOTAL FAT; 6 G SATURATED FAT; 0 MG CHOLESTEROL; 34 MG SODIUM

COOKS' TIP:

The cheese is easier to slice into strips and insert into the figs when it is cold, but it will melt faster if it is room temperature. All the better; you can prep the figs in the afternoon and set them aside until cooking, just before serving.

PREP TIME: 5 MINUTES   COOKING TIME: 2 MINUTES

Vanilla-Sugared Apricots

MAKES 4 SERVINGS

The crust of caramelized sugar is nice over apricots because they are usually tart if firm.

8 firm apricots, halved and pitted
4 tablespoons butter, melted
vanilla seeds from 1 vanilla bean
1/3 cup sugar
oil for the grill
vanilla ice cream or coconut sorbet, for serving

• Prepare a grill for barbecuing. Place the apricots on a foil-lined baking sheet and brush with the melted butter. Combine the vanilla seeds and sugar in a shallow bowl. Dip the cut side of the apricots in the vanilla sugar; shake off excess and pat the sugar onto the apricots.

• Oil the grill and a grill rack. Cook the apricots cut side down over hot heat 1 minute. Turn and cook on rounded side about 45 seconds. Serve warm with ice cream.

PER SERVING WITH 1 PINT VANILLA ICE CREAM: 333 CALORIES;
3 G PROTEIN; 40 G CARBOHYDRATES; 19 G TOTAL FAT; 12 G SATURATED FAT;
60 MG CHOLESTEROL; 171 MG SODIUM

COOKS' TIP:

You can use fine or coarse raw sugar or brown sugar instead of vanilla sugar.

PREP TIME: 10 MINUTES   COOKING TIME: 5 MINUTES

Grilled Butterscotch Pineapple

MAKES 6 SERVINGS

1 peeled, cored fresh pineapple
1/2 cup butterscotch-flavored schnapps
oil for the grill

• Prepare a grill for barbecuing. Line a baking sheet with foil. Cut pineapple crosswise into 3/4-inch thick rings. Drizzle pineapple with schnapps and turn to coat.

• Brush grill with oil. Grill pineapple over hot coals until caramelized on all sides, about 5 minutes in all.

PER SERVING: 132 CALORIES; 0 G PROTEIN; 19 G CARBOHYDRATES;
2 G TOTAL FAT; 0 G SATURATED FAT; 0 MG CHOLESTEROL; 2 MG SODIUM

Nutty Bananas

MAKES 4 SERVINGS

The bananas should be firm, but ripe. Finger bananas are also fun to use.

1/4 cup shredded coconut
1/4 cup chopped macadamia nuts
2 tablespoons canned dulce de leche or sweetened condensed milk
1 1/2 teaspoons fresh lime juice
1 1/2 teaspoons coconut rum or other flavored white rum
2 regular bananas
oil for the grill

COOKS' TIP:

You can use coconut milk instead of rum or omit the rum entirely.

• Prepare a grill for barbecuing. Mix coconut and macadamias on a plate. Soak four wooden skewers in hot water.

• Mix dulce de leche, lime juice, and rum in a cup. Peel bananas and cut into 1-inch chunks. Place on a foil-lined baking sheet and brush with the dulce de leche mixture. Roll in the coconut mixture and double skewer, with skewers parallel and cut sides of bananas facing sideways.

• Brush grill with oil. Grill over medium-low heat until bananas are hot and coconut is toasted, about 10 minutes, turning every 3 minutes.

PER SERVING: 169 CALORIES; 3 G PROTEIN; 24 G CARBOHYDRATES; 8 G TOTAL FAT; 2 G SATURATED FAT; 4 MG CHOLESTEROL; 59 MG SODIUM

Bartlett Pears with Chocolate Sauce

MAKES 4 SERVINGS

Poached pears are one of the simplest and best desserts, and grilled pears are even easier to prepare.

2 ripe and firm, but not hard, Bartlett pears
juice from 1/2 lemon
2 tablespoons canned dulce de leche or sweetened
  condensed milk
1 tablespoon pear brandy
1 tablespoon butter, melted
1/2 cup heavy cream
2 ounces bittersweet or semisweet chocolate, chopped
dried lavender or candied violets for garnish

COOKS' TIP:

Fruit is somewhat unpredictable when grilling; if the pears aren't tender after 10 minutes, keep cooking them. The crucial timing is after the glaze is applied.

- Prepare a grill for barbecuing. Cut the pears in half lengthwise. Using a melon baller or a teaspoon, scoop out the cores. Peel the pears. Working over a foil-lined baking sheet, brush the pears with lemon juice. Mix the dulce de leche, brandy, and melted butter in a small cup.

- Grill the pears, covered, over medium-low heat until lightly browned, hot, and tender, about 10 minutes.

- While the pears cook, heat the cream to boiling in the microwave or in a small saucepan. Remove from the heat, add the chocolate and whisk until melted and blended with the cream. If you need to heat it more to melt the chocolate, do it over medium-low heat.

- Brush the pear slices on the grill with the dulce de leche mixture and turn pears over. Grill 30 seconds. Turn pears over and brush with more mixture. Grill 20 to 30 seconds, until glaze caramelizes. Place the pear slices cut sides down on a cutting board and slice them lengthwise, keeping them intact at the top. Fan out pear slices on large dessert plates or in large shallow bowls and drizzle chocolate sauce around the pears. Garnish with dried lavender or candied violets.

PER SERVING: 236 CALORIES; 3 G PROTEIN; 32 G CARBOHYDRATES;
12 G TOTAL FAT; 7 G SATURATED FAT; 22 MG CHOLESTEROL; 56 MG SODIUM

PREP TIME: 10 MINUTES   COOKING TIME: 8 MINUTES

Grilled Cheese Blintzes

MAKES 4 SERVINGS

These deli classics are also darlings of the great outdoors. Who ever thought you could make them on a grill?

1 1/2 cups pineapple-flavored cottage cheese, drained,
   at room temperature
1 egg yolk
1 teaspoon vanilla extract
4 store-bought 8-inch crêpes
2 tablespoons unsalted butter, melted
oil for the grill
1/2 cup bottled pineapple sundae topping, heated

● Prepare a grill for barbecuing. In a medium bowl, mix the cottage cheese, egg yolk, and vanilla until blended. Place the crêpes on the work surface and spread 1/4 of the cottage cheese just below the center of each one. Fold the left and right sides of the crêpes partially over the filling and roll up the crêpes to form a burrito-like packet. Place on a foil-lined baking sheet and brush with the melted butter.

● Oil the grill rack and grill the blintzes over medium heat until the filling is hot, about 8 minutes, turning the blintzes every 2 minutes. Transfer the blintzes to dessert plates and drizzle with the hot sundae topping.

PER SERVING: 364 CALORIES; 12 G PROTEIN; 49 G CARBOHYDRATES;
14 G TOTAL FAT; 7 G SATURATED FAT; 101 MG CHOLESTEROL; 656 MG SODIUM

COOKS' TIP:

You can make a cheesecake-type filling by using a dollop of flavored whipped cream cheese at room-temperature instead of cottage cheese.

PREP TIME: 10 MINUTES   COOKING TIME: 3 MINUTES

Grilled Peach Melba Sundaes

MAKES 4 SERVINGS

The dessert of divas, peach Melba is even more delicious when the fruit is grilled instead of poached.

2 large ripe peaches, halved and pitted

grapeseed oil for brushing the peaches and grill

3 tablespoons sweetened condensed milk

1 tablespoon lemon-flavored vodka

pinch of cardamom

1 pint lemon gelato

1/2 pint fresh raspberries

chopped pistachios

● Prepare a grill for barbecuing. Place the peaches cut side up on a foil-lined baking sheet and brush lightly with oil. Combine the milk, vodka, and cardamom in a cup.

● Oil the grill. Place peaches cut side down on the grill and cook over high heat 1 minute. Turn peaches and grill skin side down until heated through, about 45 seconds. Brush cut sides with milk mixture and grill cut sides down until caramelized, about 30 seconds. Remove to bowls and let cool. Scoop gelato into the bowls next to the peaches and sprinkle with a few raspberries and pistachios. Serve immediately.

PER SERVING: 266 CALORIES; 4 G PROTEIN; 50 G CARBOHYDRATES;
6 G TOTAL FAT; 2 G SATURATED FAT; 11 MG CHOLESTEROL; 62 MG SODIUM

PREP TIME: 5 MINUTES   COOKING TIME: 3 MINUTES

Spiced Pink Grapefruit

MAKES 4 SERVINGS

Grilled citrus retains as much of its tangy and juicy nature as when uncooked; the real surprise is something usually served cold is hot. The acidity is a little more noticeable, too, but the Asian seasonings round out the flavor.

2 small pink grapefruits

1 tablespoon Asian sesame oil

1 teaspoon five-spice powder

3 tablespoons finely diced crystallized ginger

● Prepare a grill for barbecuing. Cut the grapefruits crosswise in half and brush cut sides with the oil. Sprinkle with the five-spice powder and grill over hot heat 1 minute. Turn 45 degrees and grill 1 minute. Turn over and grill 1 minute. Sprinkle with the crystallized ginger.

PER SERVING: 92 CALORIES; 1 G PROTEIN; 16 G CARBOHYDRATES; 4 G TOTAL
FAT; 0 G SATURATED FAT; 0 MG CHOLESTEROL; 0 MG SODIUM

COOKS' TIP:

You can peel the grapefruits and slice them into 1-inch thick rounds. Season with oil and spice mix, and grill. Sprinkle with the ginger and serve as a tasty accompaniment to grilled duck or pork.

Toasted Cake and Berries with Goat Cheese Cream

MAKES 4 SERVINGS

Grill the cake until it is hot and aromatic—it will taste freshly made.

1 *pound mixed summer berries (about 4 cups),*
   large strawberries thickly sliced
1/4 *cup orange liqueur or orange juice*
1/2 *pound chilled fresh goat cheese*
1/2 *cup heavy cream*
3 *tablespoons confectioners' sugar*
1/2 *teaspoon pure vanilla extract*
4 *slices (1/2-inch thick) pound cake*
2 *tablespoons melted butter*

• Prepare a grill for barbecuing. Mix the berries and liqueur in a bowl. Set aside.

• In a food processor, purée the cheese, cream, confectioners' sugar, and vanilla. Transfer to a bowl, cover, and refrigerate until ready to serve.

• Place the cake on a foil-lined baking sheet. Brush on both sides with butter. Grill until lightly toasted, 20 to 30 seconds; turn over and grill until golden brown, 20 to 30 seconds. Spoon the berries onto the cake and top with the goat cheese cream.

PER SERVING: 472 CALORIES; 14 G PROTEIN; 36 G CARBOHYDRATES;
27 G TOTAL FAT; 17 G SATURATED FAT; 115 MG CHOLESTEROL;
395 MG SODIUM

COOKS' TIP:

Leftover corn muffins are delicious toasted on the grill and are a nice match for the berries and cream.

Grilled Ambrosia

MAKES 6 SERVINGS

This traditional winter dessert of the American South is not without its revisions. The ingredients, toasted over a charcoal fire, are delicious any time of the year.

2 cans (11 ounces each) mandarin oranges
1 peeled, cored fresh pineapple
2 ripe but firm bananas, peeled
1 coconut
oil for the grill

• Prepare a grill for barbecuing. Line a large baking sheet with foil. Drain oranges, reserving the liquid. Place oranges in a bowl. Cut pineapple and bananas into 1-inch chunks and add to oranges.

• Crack coconut with a hammer and reserve liquid inside for another use. Remove hard shell from coconut and peel coconut pieces. Slice up coconut into 1/2-inch chunks.

• Place a hinged vegetable grilling rack on a foil-lined baking sheet and brush with oil. Pack orange segments, pineapple chunks, bananas, and coconut into rack, close rack, and secure. Grill fruits and coconut until hot and crisp, about 8 minutes in all, but turning grill rack every 1 to 2 minutes to keep fruit from burning.

• Place fruit and coconut into a bowl. Sprinkle with reserved orange juice. Serve in compote glasses.

PER SERVING: 333 CALORIES; 4 G PROTEIN; 35 G CARBOHYDRATES;
23 G TOTAL FAT; 20 G SATURATED FAT; 0 MG CHOLESTEROL;
15 MG SODIUM

Rocky Road Crêpe Torte

MAKES 8 SERVINGS

4 prepared 8-inch crêpes

4 tablespoons unsalted butter, melted

1/4 cup cinnamon sugar

2 cups miniature marshmallows

1 cup semisweet chocolate chips

1 cup chopped walnuts

oil for the grill

● Prepare a grill for barbecuing. Line a cookie sheet with foil and place a crêpe on top. Brush on the top-side with butter and sprinkle with cinnamon sugar. Turn over and repeat. Sprinkle with 1/3 of the marshmallows, chocolate chips, and walnuts and move to one side of the baking sheet. Repeat with another crêpe and place it on top of the first crêpe. Repeat with another crêpe.

● Place the last crêpe on the prepared baking sheet and brush the topside with butter. Sprinkle with cinnamon sugar and turn over. Repeat with remaining butter and cinnamon sugar. Place on top of other crêpes.

● Brush a hinged grill with oil. Place the crêpe torte in the hinged grill and cook over medium-high heat until the marshmallows and chocolate chips melt, about 8 minutes, turning torte every 2 minutes.

● Slide torte onto a cutting board and let sit 5 minutes. Cut into wedges.

PER SERVING: 653 CALORIES; 9 G PROTEIN; 70 G CARBOHYDRATES; 42 G TOTAL FAT; 17 G SATURATED FAT; 69 MG CHOLESTEROL; 42 MG SODIUM

Condiments & Brines

Maple Brine •

Apple-Cider Brine •

Pickle Brine •

Mustard-Dill Brine •

Quick Pickle-Juice Brine •

Seafood-Boil Brine •

Cuban Mojo Brine •

Asian Five-Spice Brine •

Moroccan-Spiced Brine •

Ras al Hanout (Moroccan spice mix) •

Wasabi-Soy Brine •

Sake-Ginger Brine •

Creole Brine •

Bloody Mary Brine •

Margarita Brine •

Mint Julep Brine •

Honey-Rum Brine •

Sage and Onion Brine •

Thyme and Garlic Brine •

• Rosemary and Limoncello Brine

• A l'Orange Brine

• Peking Duck Marinade

• Mexican Vanilla Brine

• Guinness Brine

• Pineapple-Pepper Relish

• Mint-Lemon Chutney

• Lemon Relish

• Cucumber Chutney

• Carrot Chutney

• Easy Mild Mango Chutney

• Quick Cooked Apple Chutney

• Spinach-Mustard Sauce

• Avocado-Olive Sauce

• Spicy Honey-Mustard Dressing

• Mrs. Ralston's Roquefort Cheese Dressing

• Chunky Tomato-Caper Ketchup

• Gomashio (Japanese sesame-seed salt)

PREP TIME: 7 MINUTES   COOKING TIME: 2 MINUTES

Maple Brine

MAKES 2 CUPS

This brine is a good choice to tenderize and flavor thick pork chops, pork tenderloin, pork loin, Cornish hens, duck, and chicken thighs.

1/2 cup water

2 whole cloves

2 whole allspice berries

2 tablespoons kosher salt

2 tablespoons pure maple syrup

1 tablespoon distilled white vinegar

12 ice cubes

● Heat water, cloves, allspice berries, salt, and syrup in a small saucepan until boiling, stirring to dissolve salt. Boil 1 minute. Pour into a heat-proof glass measure or shallow heat-proof glass baking dish. Cool 5 minutes; stir in vinegar and ice cubes.

PER TABLESPOON: 3 CALORIES; 0 G PROTEIN; 1 G CARBOHYDRATE;
0 G TOTAL FAT; 0 MG CHOLESTEROL; 436 MG SODIUM

PREP TIME: 10 MINUTES

Apple-Cider Brine

MAKES 2 CUPS

This brine is a good choice to tenderize and flavor thick pork chops, pork tenderloin, and pork loin.

3 tablespoons spiced apple-cider mix or Russian tea mix

2 tablespoons kosher salt

1/2 cup boiling water

1 tablespoon cider vinegar

12 ice cubes

● Place spiced cider mix and salt in a heat-proof glass measure or shallow heat-proof glass baking dish. Add boiling water and stir until spiced cider mix and salt are dissolved. Cool 5 minutes; stir in vinegar and ice cubes.

PER TABLESPOON: 3 CALORIES; 0 G PROTEIN; 1 G CARBOHYDRATE;
0 G TOTAL FAT; 0 MG CHOLESTEROL; 442 MG SODIUM

Pickle Brine

MAKES 2 CUPS

This brine is a good choice to tenderize and flavor thick pork chops, pork tenderloin, pork cutlets, cubed pork for kebabs, and thick pieces of salmon.

1/2 cup water

2 tablespoons pickling spice

2 tablespoons kosher salt

2 tablespoons sugar

1 tablespoon wine vinegar

12 ice cubes

• Heat water, pickling spice, salt, and sugar in a small saucepan until boiling, stirring to dissolve salt and sugar. Boil 1 minute. Pour into a heat-proof glass measure or shallow heat-proof glass baking dish. Cool 5 minutes; stir in vinegar and ice cubes.

PER TABLESPOON: 3 CALORIES; 0 G PROTEIN; 1 G CARBOHYDRATE;
0 G TOTAL FAT; 0 MG CHOLESTEROL; 436 MG SODIUM

Mustard-Dill Brine

MAKES 2 CUPS

This brine is a good choice to tenderize and flavor thick pieces of salmon, lamb, and pork.

2 tablespoons kosher salt

1 tablespoon sugar

1/2 cup boiling water

1 tablespoon Dijon mustard

1 cup snipped fresh dill

12 ice cubes

• Place salt and sugar in a heat-proof glass measure or shallow heat-proof glass baking dish. Add the boiling water and stir until salt and sugar dissolve. Cool 5 minutes; whisk in mustard and dill until mustard is blended. Stir in ice cubes.

PER TABLESPOON: 2 CALORIES; 0 G PROTEIN; 1 G CARBOHYDRATE;
0 G TOTAL FAT; 0 MG CHOLESTEROL; 442 MG SODIUM

Quick Pickle-Juice Brine

MAKES 2 CUPS

This brine is a good choice to tenderize and flavor thick pork chops, pork tenderloin, pork cutlets, cubed pork for kebabs, and thick pieces of salmon.

*1 cup pickle juice from pickles of your choice
    (sweet, sour, dill, hot cherry or jalapeño peppers,
    hot okra, etc.)*
1 cup water

- Mix pickle juice and water in a glass measure or shallow glass baking dish.

**PER TABLESPOON: 3 CALORIES; 0 G PROTEIN; 1 G CARBOHYDRATE;
0 G TOTAL FAT; 0 MG CHOLESTEROL; 436 MG SODIUM**

Seafood-Boil Brine

MAKES 2 CUPS

This brine is a good choice to tenderize and flavor shrimp, scallops, thick pieces of salmon and catfish, thick pork chops, pork tenderloin, and pork loin.

2 tablespoons kosher salt
1/2 cup boiling water
1 tablespoon Maryland-style seafood spice mix
12 ice cubes

- Place salt in a heat-proof glass measure or shallow heat-proof glass baking dish. Add the boiling water and stir until salt dissolves. Cool 5 minutes; whisk in the spice mix. Stir in ice cubes.

**PER TABLESPOON: 1 CALORIE; 0 G PROTEIN; 0 G CARBOHYDRATES;
0 G TOTAL FAT; 0 MG CHOLESTEROL; 436 MG SODIUM**

Cuban Mojo Brine

MAKES 2 CUPS

This brine is a good choice to tenderize and flavor thick pork chops, pork tenderloin, pork loin, beef roasts (such as eye roast, but it requires longer marinating and cooking), or cubes of beef for kebabs.

2 tablespoons kosher salt

2 tablespoons sugar

1/2 cup boiling water

1/2 cup cilantro leaves

1/2 cup fresh or bottled sour-orange juice or 1/4 cup each fresh orange juice and lime juice

2 cloves roasted garlic (recipe on page 165), mashed to a paste

1 teaspoon ground cumin

8 ice cubes

• Place salt and sugar in a heat-proof glass measure or shallow heat-proof glass baking dish. Add the boiling water and stir until salt and sugar dissolve. Cool 5 minutes; whisk in the cilantro, juice, garlic, and cumin until blended. Stir in ice cubes.

PER TABLESPOON: 5 CALORIES; 0 G PROTEIN; 1 G CARBOHYDRATE; 0 G TOTAL FAT; 0 MG CHOLESTEROL; 437 MG SODIUM

Asian Five-Spice Brine

MAKES 2 CUPS

This brine is a good choice to tenderize and flavor thick pork chops, pork tenderloin, pork loin, and cubed pork or chicken for kebabs.

2 tablespoons kosher salt

2 tablespoons brown sugar

1/2 cup boiling water

1 teaspoon five-spice powder

12 ice cubes

• Place salt and brown sugar in a heat-proof glass measure or shallow heat-proof glass baking dish. Add the boiling water and stir until salt and sugar dissolve. Cool 5 minutes; whisk in the spice powder. Stir in ice cubes.

PER TABLESPOON: 2 CALORIES; 0 G PROTEIN; 1 G CARBOHYDRATE; 0 G TOTAL FAT; 0 MG CHOLESTEROL; 436 MG SODIUM

PREP TIME: 10 MINUTES

Moroccan-Spiced Brine

MAKES 2 CUPS

This brine is a good choice to tenderize and flavor thick lamb chops, cubed lamb for kebabs, and ground lamb patties or meatballs.

2 tablespoons kosher salt
1/2 cup boiling water
2 teaspoons ras al hanout (Moroccan spice mix),
    recipe follows
12 ice cubes

● Place salt in a heat-proof glass measure or shallow heat-proof glass baking dish. Add the boiling water and stir until salt dissolves. Cool 5 minutes; whisk in the spice mix. Stir in ice cubes.

PER TABLESPOON: 0.4 CALORIES; 0 G PROTEIN; 0 G CARBOHYDRATES; 0 G TOTAL FAT; 0 MG CHOLESTEROL; 436 MG SODIUM

PREP TIME: 5 MINUTES

Ras al Hanout (Moroccan spice mix)

MAKES 2 TEASPOONS

This mixture is traditionally used to flavor thick lamb chops, cubed lamb for kebabs, and ground lamb patties or meatballs.

1/2 teaspoon ground cumin
1/4 teaspoon ground cardamom
1/4 teaspoon ground allspice
1/4 teaspoon freshly ground pepper
1/4 teaspoon ground ginger
1/4 teaspoon cayenne pepper
1/4 teaspoon cinnamon

● Mix ingredients in a small bowl.

PER TEASPOON: 6 CALORIES; 0 G PROTEIN; 1 G CARBOHYDRATES; 0 G TOTAL FAT; 0 MG CHOLESTEROL; 1 MG SODIUM

Wasabi-Soy Brine

MAKES 2 CUPS

This brine is a good choice to tenderize and flavor shrimp, scallops, and thick pieces of salmon and tuna.

1 tablespoon wasabi powder

1 tablespoon sugar

1/4 cup boiling water

1/4 cup soy sauce

12 ice cubes

● Place the wasabi powder and sugar in a heat-proof glass measure or shallow heat-proof glass baking dish and mix well. Add the boiling water and stir until sugar dissolves. Cool 5 minutes; whisk in the soy sauce. Stir in ice cubes.

PER TABLESPOON: 4 CALORIES; 0 G PROTEIN; 1 G CARBOHYDRATE;
0 G TOTAL FAT; 0 MG CHOLESTEROL; 129 MG SODIUM

Sake-Ginger Brine

MAKES 2 CUPS

This brine is a good choice to tenderize and flavor shrimp, scallops, and thick pieces of salmon and tuna.

1 tablespoon salt

2 teaspoons sugar

1/4 cup boiling water

1 tablespoon soy sauce

2 tablespoons sake

2 tablespoons grated fresh gingerroot

12 ice cubes

● Place the salt and sugar in a heat-proof glass measure or shallow heat-proof glass baking dish. Add the boiling water and stir until salt and sugar dissolve. Cool 5 minutes; whisk in the soy sauce, sake, and gingerroot. Stir in ice cubes.

PER TABLESPOON: 2 CALORIES; 0 G PROTEIN; 0 G CARBOHYDRATES;
0 G TOTAL FAT; 0 MG CHOLESTEROL; 250 MG SODIUM

Creole Brine

MAKES 2 CUPS

This brine is a good choice to tenderize and flavor shrimp and thick pieces of salmon and pork.

1 1/2 tablespoons kosher salt

2 teaspoons celery salt

1/2 cup boiling water

2 teaspoons freshly ground black pepper

2 teaspoons garlic powder

2 teaspoons dried oregano leaves

2 teaspoons paprika

1 teaspoon cayenne pepper

12 ice cubes

• Place the kosher salt and celery salt in a heat-proof glass measure or shallow heat-proof glass baking dish. Add the boiling water and stir until salts dissolve. Cool 5 minutes; whisk in the black pepper, garlic powder, oregano, paprika, and cayenne. Stir in ice cubes.

PER TABLESPOON: 2 CALORIES; 0 G PROTEIN; 0 G CARBOHYDRATES; 0 G TOTAL FAT; 0 MG CHOLESTEROL; 400 MG SODIUM

Bloody Mary Brine

MAKES 2 CUPS

This brine is a good choice to tenderize and flavor shrimp, thick pieces of pork and veal, and boneless chicken breasts.

1 tablespoon kosher salt

1/4 cup boiling water

1 1/4 cups Bloody Mary mix

1/4 cup pepper-flavored vodka

2 tablespoons fresh lime or lemon juice

1 tablespoon freshly grated or drained prepared horseradish

1 teaspoon Worcestershire sauce

• Place the kosher salt in a heat-proof glass measure or shallow heat-proof glass baking dish. Add the boiling water and stir until salt dissolves. Cool 5 minutes; whisk in the Bloody Mary mix, vodka, lime juice, horseradish, and Worcestershire sauce.

PER TABLESPOON: 6 CALORIES; 0 G PROTEIN; 1 G CARBOHYDRATE; 0 G TOTAL FAT; 0 MG CHOLESTEROL; 265 MG SODIUM

Margarita Brine

MAKES 2 CUPS

This brine is a good choice to tenderize and flavor shrimp, thick pieces of catfish and pork, and boneless chicken breasts.

2 tablespoons kosher salt
1/4 cup boiling water
1/4 cup bottled margarita mix or 2 tablespoons water and 2 tablespoons sweetened lime juice
2 tablespoons tequila
12 ice cubes

● Place the kosher salt in a heat-proof glass measure or shallow heat-proof glass baking dish. Add the boiling water and stir until salt dissolves. Cool 5 minutes; whisk in the margarita mix and tequila. Stir in ice cubes.

PER TABLESPOON: 3 CALORIES; 0 G PROTEIN; 0 G CARBOHYDRATES; 0 G TOTAL FAT; 0 MG CHOLESTEROL; 438 MG SODIUM

Mint Julep Brine

MAKES 2 CUPS

This brine is a good choice to tenderize and flavor thick pork chops, pork tenderloin, and pork loin.

2 tablespoons kosher salt
2 tablespoons sugar
1/4 cup boiling water
1 cup mint leaves
2 tablespoons bourbon
12 ice cubes

● Place the kosher salt and sugar in a heat-proof glass measure or shallow heat-proof glass baking dish. Add the boiling water and stir until salt and sugar dissolve. Cool 5 minutes; whisk in the mint and bourbon. Stir in ice cubes.

PER TABLESPOON: 6 CALORIES; 0 G PROTEIN; 1 G CARBOHYDRATE; 0 G TOTAL FAT; 0 MG CHOLESTEROL; 436 MG SODIUM

Honey-Rum Brine

MAKES 2 CUPS

This brine is a good choice to tenderize and flavor thick pieces of pork, Cornish hens, and boneless chicken thighs and breasts.

2 tablespoons kosher salt
2 tablespoons honey
1/4 cup boiling water
2 tablespoons spiced rum or plain dark or light rum
12 ice cubes

● Place the kosher salt and honey in a heat-proof glass measure or shallow heat-proof glass baking dish. Add the boiling water and stir until salt and honey dissolve. Cool 5 minutes; whisk in the rum. Stir in ice cubes.

PER TABLESPOON: 6 CALORIES; 0 G PROTEIN; 1 G CARBOHYDRATE; 0 G TOTAL FAT; 0 MG CHOLESTEROL; 436 MG SODIUM

Sage and Onion Brine

MAKES 2 CUPS

This brine is a good choice to tenderize and flavor shrimp, thick pieces of pork and veal, turkey cutlets, and boneless chicken breasts.

2 tablespoons kosher salt
1/2 cup boiling water
1/4 cup grated onion
1/2 teaspoon cracked peppercorns
1/2 cup loosely packed sage leaves
12 ice cubes

● Place the kosher salt in a heat-proof glass measure or shallow heat-proof glass baking dish. Add the boiling water and stir until salt dissolves. Cool 5 minutes; whisk in the onion, peppercorns, and sage. Stir in ice cubes.

PER TABLESPOON: 2 CALORIES; 0 G PROTEIN; 0.5 G CARBOHYDRATE; 0 G TOTAL FAT; 0 MG CHOLESTEROL; 436 MG SODIUM

Thyme and Garlic Brine

MAKES 2 CUPS

This brine is a good choice to tenderize and flavor thick pieces of pork, veal, lamb, beef steaks, and boneless chicken breasts.

2 tablespoons kosher salt

1/2 cup boiling water

6 garlic cloves, crushed through a press

1 bunch fresh thyme sprigs or 1 tablespoon dried thyme leaves

12 ice cubes

● Place the kosher salt in a heat-proof glass measure or shallow heat-proof glass baking dish. Add the boiling water and stir until salt dissolves. Cool 5 minutes; whisk in the garlic and thyme. Stir in ice cubes.

PER TABLESPOON: 1 CALORIE; 0 G PROTEIN; 0 G CARBOHYDRATES; 0 G TOTAL FAT; 0 MG CHOLESTEROL; 436 MG SODIUM

Rosemary and Limoncello Brine

MAKES 2 CUPS

This brine is a good choice to tenderize and flavor shrimp, thick pieces of pork, and boneless chicken breasts.

2 tablespoons kosher salt

1/2 cup boiling water

2 rosemary sprigs (8 inches each), cut in half

1/4 cup limoncello (Italian lemon liqueur) or 1/4 cup water, 2 tablespoons sugar, and the zest of 1 lemon

8 ice cubes

● Place the kosher salt in a heat-proof glass measure or shallow heat-proof glass baking dish. Add the boiling water and stir until salt dissolves. Cool 5 minutes; whisk in the rosemary and limoncello. Stir in ice cubes.

PER TABLESPOON: 8 CALORIES; 0 G PROTEIN; 1 G CARBOHYDRATE; 0 G TOTAL FAT; 0 MG CHOLESTEROL; 436 MG SODIUM

A l'Orange Brine

MAKES 2 CUPS

This brine is a good choice to tenderize and flavor shrimp, thick pieces of pork, duck breasts, Cornish hens, and boneless chicken thighs and breasts.

2 tablespoons kosher salt
1/2 cup boiling water
1/4 cup Grand Marnier or other orange liqueur
2 tablespoons fresh orange juice
2 tablespoons fresh lemon juice
8 ice cubes

• Place the kosher salt in a heat-proof glass measure or shallow heat-proof glass baking dish. Add the boiling water and stir until salt dissolves. Cool 5 minutes; whisk in the liqueur and juices. Stir in ice cubes.

PER TABLESPOON: 8 CALORIES; 0 G PROTEIN; 1 G CARBOHYDRATE;
0 G TOTAL FAT; 0 MG CHOLESTEROL; 436 MG SODIUM

Peking Duck Marinade

MAKES 2 CUPS

This brine is a good choice to tenderize and flavor shrimp in the shell, thick pieces of pork, duck breasts, Cornish hens, and boneless chicken thighs and breasts.

1 tablespoon kosher salt
1/3 cup boiling water
2 tablespoons hoisen sauce
1 cup finely chopped scallions
12 ice cubes

• Place the kosher salt in a heat-proof glass measure or shallow heat-proof glass baking dish. Add the boiling water and stir until salt dissolves. Whisk in the hoisen sauce until blended. Cool 5 minutes; whisk in the scallions. Stir in ice cubes.

PER TABLESPOON: 4 CALORIES; 0 G PROTEIN; 1 G CARBOHYDRATE;
0 G TOTAL FAT; 0 MG CHOLESTEROL; 237 MG SODIUM

Mexican Vanilla Brine

MAKES 2 CUPS

This brine is a good choice to tenderize and flavor thick pieces of salmon and pork and infuse lobster tails or scallops before grilling.

2 tablespoons kosher salt

2 tablespoons sugar

1 tablespoon cracked black peppercorns

1/2 cup boiling water

12 ice cubes

2 tablespoons pure Mexican vanilla extract or other
    vanilla extract

• Place salt, sugar, and peppercorns in a heat-proof glass measure or shallow heat-proof glass baking dish. Add the boiling water and stir until salt and sugar dissolve. Stir in the ice cubes and cool 5 minutes. Stir in the vanilla.

**PER TABLESPOON: 5 CALORIES; 0 G PROTEIN; 1 G CARBOHYDRATE;
0 G TOTAL FAT; 0 MG CHOLESTEROL; 436 MG SODIUM**

Guinness Brine

MAKES 2 CUPS

This hearty liquid can be used to enrich the flavor of grilled beef and venison.

2 tablespoons kosher salt

1 tablespoon sugar

1/4 cup boiling water

1 bottle (12 ounces) Guinness stout

• Place salt and sugar in a heat-proof glass measure. Add the boiling water and stir until salt and sugar dissolve. Pour the brine into a shallow heat-proof glass baking dish. Stir in the Guinness stout.

**PER TABLESPOON: 6 CALORIES; 0 G PROTEIN; 1 G CARBOHYDRATE;
0 G TOTAL FAT; 0 MG CHOLESTEROL; 437 MG SODIUM**

PREP TIME: 10 MINUTES

Pineapple-Pepper Relish

MAKES 6 SERVINGS, ABOUT 1 1/2 CUPS

This is a tasty mix to serve with grilled fish, shrimp, ham steaks, and pork.

1 can (4 ounces) chopped jalapeños
1 jar (4 ounces) chopped pimientos
1 can (8 ounces) crushed pineapple in natural juices
1/4 cup fresh cilantro leaves, chopped
1 tablespoon grated fresh gingerroot
fresh lime juice to taste

● Drain jalapeños, pimientos, and pineapple (reserve the juices to use in marinades if desired) and place in a bowl. Stir in enough of the reserved jalapeño or pineapple juices to make a juicy but not soupy mixture. Stir in the cilantro, gingerroot, and lime juice.

PER SERVING: 35 CALORIES; 1 G PROTEIN; 9 G CARBOHYDRATES; 1 G TOTAL FAT; 0 G SATURATED FAT; 0 MG CHOLESTEROL; 321 MG SODIUM

PREP TIME: 10 MINUTES

Mint-Lemon Chutney

MAKES 8 SERVINGS

This mix is traditionally served with grilled lamb kebabs for dipping.

juice of 2 lemons
4 hot green chiles, such as jalapeños, stems and seeds removed
2 garlic cloves, sliced
1 cup packed fresh mint leaves
1/4 cup chopped onion
1 tablespoon chopped peeled fresh gingerroot
2 teaspoons sugar

● Combine ingredients in a blender or food processor and pulse until combined. Blend or process until smooth.

PER SERVING: 16 CALORIES; 0 G PROTEIN; 4 G CARBOHYDRATES; 0 G TOTAL FAT; 0 MG CHOLESTEROL; 2 MG SODIUM

PREP TIME: 15 MINUTES, PLUS REFRIGERATION

Lemon Relish

MAKES 6 SERVINGS, ABOUT 1¹/2 CUPS

Match a bite of this mixture per bite of grilled meats and poultry and you have a winning combination. Season the relish with Tabasco sauce instead of using a fresh chile if you want.

2 *large lemons*

6 *fat scallions, with healthy green tops, trimmed and*
   cut into 1-inch pieces

1 *cup chopped celery*

¹/2 *cup chopped green bell pepper*

¹/4 *cup packed parsley leaves*

1 *small hot red chile, seeded and chopped*

1 *tablespoon sugar*

1 *teaspoon salt*

¹/2 *teaspoon dry mustard powder*

¹/4 *teaspoon ground cardamom*

● Grate the zest from the lemons and set aside in a large bowl. Remove the white pith from the lemons with a paring knife and cut the lemons into quarters. Remove and discard the seeds. Place the lemons in a food processor and process until evenly chopped. Add the scallions, celery, bell pepper, and parsley and process until coarsely and evenly chopped.

● Scrape the relish into the bowl with the grated lemon zest and stir in the red chile, sugar, salt, mustard, and cardamom. Mix well. Cover and refrigerate overnight if possible to allow the flavors to ripen.

PER SERVING: 33 CALORIES; 1 G PROTEIN; 10 G CARBOHYDRATES; 1 G TOTAL
FAT; 0 G SATURATED FAT; 0 MG CHOLESTEROL; 409 MG SODIUM

Cucumber Chutney

MAKES 8 SERVINGS

Here's a delicious "sauce" to serve with grilled kebabs of any type. It's best to serve soon after making so the salt doesn't make the cucumbers and onions watery.

*1 pound English or Kirby cucumbers, trimmed
   and peeled*
*1 pound Vidalia onions or other sweet onions,
   peeled and finely chopped*
2 garlic cloves, minced (optional)
1 tablespoon chopped fresh cilantro (optional)
1 teaspoon salt
*1/2 teaspoon freshly ground black pepper or
   chili powder*
juice of 1 lemon

● Slice cucumbers lengthwise and use a teaspoon to scrape out the seeds. Finely chop the cucumbers and place in a bowl. Add the onions, garlic, cilantro, salt, pepper, and lemon juice. Mix well.

PER SERVING (WITH GARLIC AND CILANTRO): 32 CALORIES; 1 G PROTEIN; 1 G CARBOHYDRATE; 1 G TOTAL FAT; 0 G SATURATED FAT; 0 MG CHOLESTEROL; 292 MG SODIUM

Carrot Chutney

MAKES 6 SERVINGS

This sweet, tangy, and colorful mixture will liven up a platter of grilled meat or poultry. Offer it as an alternative to sauerkraut for topping grilled sausages or hot dogs!

1 bag (8 ounces) peeled baby carrots
1 bunch thin scallions, chopped (1/3 cup)
juice of 1 lemon
2 tablespoons chopped fresh cilantro
1 tablespoon grated peeled fresh gingerroot
1 teaspoon salt

● Place carrots in a food processor and process until evenly chopped (the pieces should be fine but do not purée). Place in a bowl and add the scallions, lemon juice, cilantro, gingeroot, and salt. Fold gently until mixed.

PER SERVING: 22 CALORIES; 1 G PROTEIN; 5 G CARBOHYDRATES; 0 G TOTAL FAT; 0 MG CHOLESTEROL; 400 MG SODIUM

Easy Mild Mango Chutney

MAKES 12 SERVINGS

This is delicious with curry-flavored grilled dishes as part of the traditional accompaniments: saffron rice, chopped nuts, pickles, fresh chutney, and shredded coconut.

1/2 teapoon ground allspice

1/2 teaspoon ground ginger

1/2 teaspoon ground cumin

1 tablespoon peanut or olive oil

1/4 teaspoon brown mustard seeds

1/4 teaspoon kaloinji (nigella) seeds or caraway seeds

1/4 teaspoon cumin seeds

1/4 teaspoon fennel seeds

1 can (18 ounces) mango chunks in extra-heavy syrup

● Heat the ground spices in a small nonstick skillet over medium heat until fragrant, about 2 minutes. Pour into a small bowl. Heat the oil in the same skillet until hot; add mustard seeds. Immediately cover the skillet and remove the pan from heat. When the popping has stopped, add remaining seeds; cover and return to heat. Cook, shaking skillet gently, 1 minute. Remove from heat. When the seeds are quiet, remove the lid and stir in the roasted spices and about 1/2 cup of the syrup from the mangos. Heat the syrup over medium-high heat and simmer 10 minutes.

● While the syrup simmers, drain the remaining mango syrup into a 2-quart saucepan. Dice the mango pieces into 1/2-inch chunks and add to the pan. Heat to boiling and stir in the spiced syrup. Simmer the chutney over medium heat until thick, stirring frequently as the syrup reduces, about 15 minutes. Cool and spoon into jars. Store in the refrigerator.

PER SERVING: 47 CALORIES; 0 G PROTEIN; 9 G CARBOHYDRATES; 1 G TOTAL FAT; 0 G SATURATED FAT; 0 MG CHOLESTEROL; 8 MG SODIUM

PREP TIME: 10 MINUTES   COOKING TIME: 20 MINUTES

Quick Cooked Apple Chutney

MAKES 12 SERVINGS

A dollop of this spicy fruit relish is all you need to enhance the flavor of grilled pork, duck, or chicken. It also makes a tasty partner with a block of softened cream cheese for hors d'oeuvres. Top the cream cheese with the chutney and let guests spread the mixture over whole-grain crackers or celery sticks.

1 can (15.75 ounces) apple pie filling with cinnamon and spices

1 small Vidalia or other sweet onion, grated

1 large garlic clove, crushed through a press

1 cup distilled white vinegar or red wine vinegar

2 tablespoons yellow mustard seeds

1 tablespoon ground ginger

1/4 teaspoon ground turmeric

1/4 teaspoon crushed red pepper flakes

1/2 cup raisins

● Combine ingredients except raisins in a stainless steel or an enamel-lined saucepan. Heat over medium heat, stirring occasionally with a wooden spoon, until boiling. Simmer over medium-low heat, stirring more often as mixture thickens and breaking up apples into smaller pieces, until almost all the liquid has evaporated, about 20 minutes. Stir in raisins and let cool. Spoon into jars and store in the refrigerator.

PER SERVING: 72 CALORIES; 1 G PROTEIN; 17 G CARBOHYDRATES; 1 G TOTAL FAT; 0 G SATURATED FAT; 0 MG CHOLESTEROL; 18 MG SODIUM

Spinach-Mustard Sauce

MAKES 4 SERVINGS

This makes a great topping for grilled steaks, lamb, salmon, and chicken. You can use it as a dip with grilled pita, and it makes a tangy dressing for vegetable salads.

1 package (10 ounces) frozen chopped spinach,
 thawed
1/2 cup fat-free sour cream
1/2 cup fat-free plain yogurt
3 tablespoons Dijon mustard
1 tablespoon chopped fresh dill
fresh lemon juice to taste
freshly ground pepper to taste

● Spread out the spinach on a rimless dinner plate and place another plate on top. Press the plates over the sink so the spinach water drips out. (Squeezing the spinach between two plates removes the water but doesn't pack the spinach as much as if you squeezed it in your hands.)

● Scrape the spinach into a bowl and add the sour cream, yogurt, mustard, and dill. Taste and season with lemon juice and pepper.

PER SERVING: 83 CALORIES; 5 G PROTEIN; 8 G CARBOHYDRATES; 0 G TOTAL FAT; 0 MG CHOLESTEROL; 220 MG SODIUM

Avocado-Olive Sauce

MAKES 4 SERVINGS

This glamorized guacamole is perfect alongside any kind of grilled fish or shrimp. It makes a great dressing for grilled chicken or seafood salads.

1 ripe avocado, peeled, pitted, and cubed
1 cup fat-free sour cream or yogurt
4 teaspoons fresh lime juice
2 tablespoons chopped fresh cilantro
1/2 teaspoon salt
1/4 cup sliced pitted black olives
1 jar (2 ounces) chopped pimientos, drained

● Place avocado in a food processor and add the sour cream, lime juice, cilantro, and salt. Process until blended and smooth. Scrape into a bowl and stir in the olives and pimientos.

PER SERVING: 130 CALORIES; 5 G PROTEIN; 10 G CARBOHYDRATES; 9 G TOTAL FAT; 1 G SATURATED FAT; 1 MG CHOLESTEROL; 417 MG SODIUM

Spicy Honey-Mustard Dressing

MAKES 8 SERVINGS

This saucy mixture is not only for salads; it's a delicious dip for grilled or fried veggies and chicken wings and a versatile ingredient in marinades and glazes for grilling.

1/2 cup prepared mayonnaise

1/4 cup prepared yellow mustard

1/4 cup honey

2 tablespoons peanut oil

1/4 teaspoon garlic powder

1/8 teaspoon cayenne pepper

• Combine the ingredients in a bowl and whisk until blended.

PER SERVING: 125 CALORIES; 1 G PROTEIN; 13 G CARBOHYDRATES; 9 G TOTAL FAT; 1 G SATURATED FAT; 4 MG CHOLESTEROL; 192 MG SODIUM

Mrs. Ralston's Roquefort Cheese Dressing

MAKES 12 SERVINGS, ABOUT 1 QUART

This is the king of dressings—perfect for greens, crudités, and chicken wings.

8 ounces crumbled Roquefort cheese

6 ounces canned evaporated milk

juice of 1 lemon

2 cups mayonnaise

dash of celery seed

1 teaspoon garlic salt

1 tablespoon chopped fresh parsley

2 tablespoons distilled white vinegar

• Combine ingredients in a medium bowl and whisk until blended and smooth. Spoon into a jar and store in the refrigerator.

PER SERVING: 244 CALORIES; 6 G PROTEIN; 12 G CARBOHYDRATES; 20 G TOTAL FAT; 6 G SATURATED FAT; 31 MG CHOLESTEROL; 732 MG SODIUM

PREP TIME: 10 MINUTES

Chunky Tomato-Caper Ketchup

MAKES 4 SERVINGS

Like its bottled, thick cousin, this simple sauce adds a tangy bite to any grilled food, from meats to poultry, seafood, and vegetables. It's even a great topping for grilled toast or mushroom caps.

1 cup coarsely chopped ripe tomato
1/2 cup bottled Caesar salad dressing
1/4 cup finely chopped fresh parsley
2 tablespoons drained small capers
fresh lemon juice to taste

● Mix tomato, dressing, parsley, and capers in a bowl. Season with lemon juice.

PER SERVING: 150 CALORIES; 1 G PROTEIN; 6 G CARBOHYDRATES; 14 G TOTAL FAT; 2 G SATURATED FAT; 0 MG CHOLESTEROL; 365 MG SODIUM

PREP TIME: 5 MINUTES   COOKING TIME: 2 MINUTES

Gomashio (Japanese sesame-seed salt)

MAKES 8 SERVINGS

Goma is the Japanese name for sesame. This mixture is used as a table condiment to sprinkle on just about any dish, from raw vegetables to fish and salads.

2 tablespoons sesame seeds
2 teaspoons kosher salt

● Lightly toast the sesame seeds in a dry, nonstick skillet over medium heat for 1 to 2 minutes, stirring frequently. Allow seeds to cool, then grind them together with the salt in a spice mill or with mortar and pestle. Transfer to an airtight jar and store in the freezer or refrigerator.

PER SERVING: 13 CALORIES; 0 G PROTEIN; 1 G CARBOHYDRATES; 1 G TOTAL FAT; 0.5 G SATURATED; 0 MG CHOLESTEROL; 578 MG SODIUM

COOKS' TIP:

Sesame seeds sold in spice-rack bottles are shockingly expensive. You can find sesame seeds in economical amounts in Asian food stores so you can make up 1-cup batches of the mix at a time.

Metric Equivalents

The recipes that appear in this cookbook use the standard United States method for measuring liquid and dry or solid ingredients (teaspoons, tablespoons, and cups). The information on this chart is provided to help cooks outside the U.S. successfully use these recipes. All equivalents are approximate.

Metric Equivalents for Different Types of Ingredients

A standard cup measure of a dry or solid ingredient will vary in weight depending on the type of ingredient. A standard cup of liquid is the same volume for any type of liquid. Use the following chart when converting standard cup measures to grams (weight) or milliliters (volume).

Standard Cup	Fine Powder (e.g. flour)	Grain (e.g. rice)	Granular (e.g. sugar)	Liquid Solids (e.g. butter)	Liquid (e.g. milk)
1	140 g	150 g	190 g	200 g	240 ml
$3/4$	105 g	113 g	143 g	150 g	180 ml
$2/3$	93 g	100 g	125 g	133 g	160 ml
$1/2$	70 g	75 g	95 g	100 g	120 ml
$1/3$	47 g	50 g	63 g	67 g	80 ml
$1/4$	35 g	38 g	48 g	50 g	60 ml
$1/8$	18 g	19 g	24 g	25 g	30 ml

Useful Equivalents for Liquid Ingredients By Volume

$1/4$ tsp =				1 ml
$1/2$ tsp =				2 ml
1 tsp =				5 ml
3 tsp =	1 tbls =		$1/2$ fl oz =	15 ml
	2 tbls =	$1/8$ cup =	1 fl oz =	30 ml
	4 tbls =	$1/4$ cup =	2 fl oz =	60 ml
	$5^1/3$ tbls =	$1/3$ cup =	3 fl oz =	80 ml
	8 tbls =	$1/2$ cup =	4 fl oz =	120 ml
	$10^2/3$ tbls =	$2/3$ cup =	5 fl oz =	160 ml
	12 tbls =	$3/4$ cup =	6 fl oz =	180 ml
	16 tbls =	1 cup =	8 fl oz =	240 ml
	1 pt =	2 cups =	16 fl oz =	480 ml
	1 qt =	4 cups =	32 fl oz =	960 ml
			33 fl oz =	1000 ml = 1l

Useful Equivalents For Dry Ingredients By Weight

(To convert ounces to grams, multiply the number of ounces by 30.)

1 oz	=	$1/16$ lb	=	30 g
4 oz	=	$1/4$ lb	=	120 g
8 oz	=	$1/2$ lb	=	240 g
12 oz	=	$3/4$ lb	=	360 g
16 oz	=	1 lb	=	480 g

Useful Equivalents for Length

(To convert inches to centimeters, multiply the number of inches by 2.5.)

1 in =				2.5 cm
6 in =	$1/2$ ft =			15 cm
12 in =	1 ft =			30 cm
36 in =	3 ft =	1 yd =	90 cm
40 in =				100 cm = 1 m

Useful Equivalents for Cooking/Oven Temperatures

	Fahrenheit	Celsius	Gas Mark
Freeze Water	32° F	0° C	
Room Temperature	68° F	20° C	
Boil Water	212° F	100° C	
Bake	325° F	160° C	3
	350° F	180° C	4
	375° F	190° C	5
	400° F	200° C	6
	425° F	220° C	7
	450° F	230° C	8
Broil			Grill

Index